THE SECRET TO REAL ESTATE

INVESTING

THE SECRET TO REAL ESTATE INVESTING

INVESTING

How to Find Your Path Through the
Real Estate Investor Maze

JOE LOCKLEAR & ADAM LOCKLEAR

The Secret to Real Estate Investing

How to Find Your Path Through the Real Estate Investor Maze

This book and the stories contained herein should not be solely relied upon when making personal investment decisions. Every individual or company has a different situation, business plan, and financial responsibilities. It is up to you to seek the proper investment advice from a qualified investment broker who can counsel you personally and to obtain legal counsel from a competent attorney who practices law in your jurisdiction.

Cover and Interior design by Caroline Johnson

Printed in the United States of America

First Printing, 2017

ISBN 978-0-9995085-0-3 (Paperback)

ISBN 978-0-9995085-1-0 (E-book)

Millcove Publishing

Jacksonville, FL

This book is dedicated to our wives. Without their constant love, sacrifice, and support, we surely would not have been able to reach any level of success. You enrich our lives and pick us up when we hit the ground.From the bottom of our hearts, thank you!

Introduction

Who is Joe Locklear and why should I read his book?

Joe Locklear is a pioneer of Jacksonville, Florida real estate investing. His accomplishments include over 700 residential investment deals and 300+ residential renovations. As past president and education director of the Jacksonville Real Estate Investors Association and the Professional Real Estate Investors Association, Joe has taught thousands of local students how to profit from buying, renovating, selling, and renting single family homes. His experience as an educator can be traced all the way back to the Robert Allen Nothing Down (RAND) Group and the American Congress of Real Estate (ACRE).

While many call Joe a "real estate guru," he sees himself more as an investor who is willing to help others. Joe will tell you that most of the "gurus" teach you very little that you can actually use. Instead, their goal is to sell you thousands of dollars in education. If they really knew the "secret" to successful investing, as they profess, then why are they selling education instead of investing? Joe likes to say that he is a "graduate of the School of Hard Knocks and a charter member of the Good Old Boys' Club." You will love his simple, honest, and direct method of teaching.

Please note that this book deals exclusively with residential single family homes.

"This won't be the usual get-rich-quick BS that you see everywhere. I make my living buying, renovating, selling, and owning

houses. I don't need to sell education, so
I will be telling you the truth—not what I think you want
to hear. This book will show you how you can determine
a *specific* path that will provide you with your best
chance of success in real estate investing."
— *Joe Locklear*

Who is Adam Locklear and why should I care what he says?

Adam has been part of the real estate investment business since he was 17. From an early age, he learned how to purchase, renovate, and rent investment homes to achieve monthly cash flow and build equity for retirement. After graduating business school, he founded his first real estate brokerage and began purchasing bank-owned properties. He built up the property management side of his real estate company before selling it in 2015.

As a wholesale expert specializing in the low to mid real estate markets, he has successfully completed more than 300 deals in the past eight years.

Having grown up around the real estate investment business, and launching his career at a young age, Adam brings considerable knowledge to the table when it comes to making a living doing deals and investing in real estate.

Foreword from Joe Locklear

Throughout my real estate investing career, I have resisted the call to reveal the secrets of my success. Now, as I near retirement, I am finally comfortable with the idea. I simply love teaching others, and I am really excited about teaching you. Whether you are just contemplating becoming involved in real estate or you're already a seasoned investor, I want to help you along your path to success.

It is important to understand that most all real estate investor education is written, promoted, and sold by what I call the "real estate gurus." The majority of these gurus' businesses are built not on buying and selling *real estate*, but on selling *education*. Most of their education is sound, but the problem is they promote a "one shoe fits all" concept. The first priority of their education is that it must be "sellable." Most never ask or answer the fundamental question: *Will it work for you?*

Having taught literally thousands of new investors over the past 30 years, it never fails to amaze me when I hear them say things like "I want to 'invest' in homes that I can sell for a good profit" or "I want to buy houses that are easy to finance." When I ask them why, I seldom get a reasonable answer. Many of these hopeful students have spent tens of thousands of dollars on real estate investing education, but they've neglected to consider the most fundamental issue. I call this commonly overlooked issue "The Secret to Real Estate Investing."

Foreword from Adam Locklear

Much of what I have learned in real estate has been through the lens of a second-generation real estate investor. Unlike many investors who quit their day jobs and plunged into doing real estate deals full time, I have had the wonderful privilege of growing up around the business.

It's true I did my first deal when I was 18. It's also true I made $11K on that deal in a week's time by flipping a mobile home. It's also true that I booked a plane ticket to Costa Rica, slept in the jungle for a month, surfed daily, and blew every red cent I had earned.

I was very fortunate growing up with a father who earned his full income doing real estate investment deals. Just to be clear, he wasn't a real estate agent who sold houses on the weekend and sup-plemented his income by doing a few investment deals on the side. He was a full-time real estate investor who earned six figures doing investment deals.

Even though my dad taught me a ton about doing deals, he didn't really teach me much about how to earn an income in real estate. He also didn't teach me about personal finances or how to run my own business.

My hope and intention for writing "Adam's Take" at the end of each chapter is to give you a different perspective on real estate investing. It's my story and thoughts as well as my insights from our family's second-generation School of Hard Knocks. Over the last 18 years, I have gained immense knowledge from hanging out with my dad, picking his brain, walking through properties with him, and analyzing deals. The information I gleaned early in my career was priceless, and it helped me develop a working business model for my current real estate investment company.

Without Joe's insights and motivation, I would never have been able to do my first deal. I also wouldn't have been able to found a company, grow that company, and eventually sell it. I am forever grateful for the time and energy he has invested in me, and I hope I can pass that knowledge on to you in this book.

Earlier in my career, I wish I had been wise and heeded others' advice about investing properly and doing deals a certain way. But I guess I am as "smart" as the rest of them. I took what Joe said with a grain of salt, and, although I learned so much from him, I ended up making my own mistakes along the way. The coolest part of our story, for me, is seeing how the next generation learns from our mistakes. If every generation passes on their knowledge to the next, and that generation follows suit, you will eventually build a dynasty.

I truly want for you to learn from our mistakes. We hope you can be our third generation of successful real estate investors. Of course, that's only if my daughters don't beat you to it. They're already showing houses as toddlers, so you'd better get started!

Contents

Section I: Choosing Your Path

Section II: Your Investor Toolbox

Section III: Sharpen Your Technical Toolbox

Section IV: Advice from Joe & Adam

SECTION I

Choosing Your Path

I shall be telling this with a sigh
Somewhere ages and ages hence:
Two roads diverged in a wood, and I—
I took the one less traveled by,
And that has made all the difference.
Robert Frost

CHAPTER 1

Taking Stock of Yourself

It has been said that every journey begins with a single step. I would add that every successful business journey begins not with a step but with careful self-analysis. I often ask this question of my students: "What is the first thing you must understand before planning any trip?" Their answer is always "where you are going."

Most of the real estate gurus would have you believe this answer is correct. They need you to focus on the destination first so they can convince you that the method they are selling is the best way for you to get there. They may get you all motivated and excited, but are they really looking out for your best interest? Almost every technique that is marketed by these gurus will work. But will it work for *you*? Now I don't blame the gurus for selling what has worked for them, but YOU will blame yourself later if you skip the most important steps in planning your investing career.

It all starts by asking yourself a few simple questions.

Where Are You?

No journey can be planned unless you understand exactly *where* the trip will begin. In other words, who are you? What are your assets and abilities? If you skip this step, your chances of success will be greatly diminished. Let's look at some basic guidelines that will help you establish your current location. You might want to make a list of all your assets and abilities. This list will be very helpful as you continue to consider your path in the real estate business.

As far as your cash assets, decide how much cash on hand you can devote to real estate operations. You should also take stock of funds in your IRA or other savings plans. Next, consider your background. What is your existing experience and areas of education and expertise? What about your personality and temperament? Do you like to move quickly, or are you more of a plodder? Do you tolerate risk well, or do you worry a lot? Be honest with yourself. I know that people do change, but your best chance of success will be to begin by maximizing *your current assets and abilities* and working within *your existing personality traits*.

Finally, you need to assess how much time you can devote to your real estate operation. Can you spend only an hour a month, or a full 40-60 hours a week? The amount of time you can devote will be a major factor in determining the paths available to you.

Where Do You Want to Go?

Once you have a solid understanding of exactly where you are, your next consideration should be *where you want to go*. You need to focus on the final destination. Wanting to be a landlord and own rental property or drive a new Porsche may be stepping stones along the path, but these are not destinations. Focus on a single destination right now. Do you just need a little extra monthly income, or is your goal to become filthy rich? Do you want to leave your existing job for a new career in real estate, or, like me, is your main goal to establish a passive income for an enjoyable retirement? I would suggest that you start with only one goal. As you gain experience and enjoy success on your beginning path, other opportunities will open themselves to you.

How Much Time Do You Have to Reach Your Destination?

Finally, you need to determine how much time you have to reach your destination. Let's say you are in Florida and need to travel to California. Without a time frame, you cannot determine your options. If you have three weeks to get there, you have a myriad of options—anything from a plane trip to hitchhiking. If, however, you only have a few hours, then you'd better book the first flight available.

Hopefully, after a bit of honest and thoughtful assessment, you will have a pretty good idea of where you are, where you want to go, and how long you have to get there. After you establish these three parameters, you are ready to take a serious second look at the common real estate investing paths. In the next few chapters, we will take a look at five popular real estate pathways. As you're reading, I want you to consider how each specific technique will fit in with YOUR assets, abilities, and time frame.

Adam's Take on Taking Stock of Yourself

I can remember the first time I sat through this class. Yes, these three simple questions pack enough content for an entire class! Joe is a great teacher, and he has helped so many students get into their best mindset—offering them the opportunity to really figure out *where* they want to go and *how* they'll get there. Since then, I have watched thousands of newbie investors sit through real estate investor classes, courses, weekend seminars, boot camps, bus tours, and countless training events. It always amazes me that every single one of them shows up with the same mentality. They want to make the big bucks, and they saw it on HGTV, so it must be true, right? Well, let's see if it's really that easy to just quit your day job, start raking in tons of cash, and sail off into the sunset like all those HGTV stars.

With that said, if anyone was going to be a multi-millionaire by the age of 30 from real estate investing, it should have been me. I am the only person I know who grew up with a father who did nothing but make money from real estate deals. It was his primary source of income, and he earned over six figures each year putting together deals and selling them to other investors. He was a full-time real estate wholesaler, and he was able to actually triple his income during a time when people were losing their day jobs and bracing for recessions. I wasn't raised to work long hours trapped in a cubicle, and I darn sure wasn't raised to break my back all day for a paycheck.

Now, I'm not saying there's anything wrong with manual labor. In my opinion, it builds character, and working with your hands is a great way to loosen up your thoughts. It's just not how I was raised to earn my living. I was taught from a young age the importance of investing my money. Forget slaving away all day to bring in a hard-earned paycheck. I was taught to invest instead. My piggy bank earned interest and yours should too. All that being said, earning a full-time, six-figure income from real estate investing and feeding my family was *leagues harder* than I ever thought it would be. Let's dig a little deeper and see what I was up against. We will use Joe's model for taking stock of yourself to see where I went wrong.

Where Was I?

This mentality really hit home for a young, pimpled 17-year-old who was eager to get started in real estate investing. At the time, I had actually been reading motivational real estate investor books from famous authors who were telling me how to get rich. I was attending local REIA meetings and had started to gain an inflated sense of confidence about real estate. It wasn't rare to find me jabbering on about how I was going to put my money to work for itself once I got into my full-time career. I knew I wanted to be rich when I grew up, and I knew by the time I was 30 I would never have to work another day in my life. The only problem with my get-rich-quick scheme was I had no idea *how* I was actually going to get there because I failed to analyze my current situation.

The reality was, I was just a broke senior in high school who barely had enough spare change to gas up my Jeep Wrangler and drive to the beach to surf and hang out with my buddies. I had no experience in sales, no real understanding of how to do deals, and no actual money saved up to buy houses. I was motivated and thirsty for knowledge, and I was somehow lucky enough to be around some really successful real estate investors. I had big dreams, but, in all honesty, I was just a knucklehead kid dreaming of wealth I had no chance of attaining—at least at that time. I soon learned I had a mountain to climb, and if I was ever going to reach any form of wealth, I was going to have to come up with a solid plan on how to get there.

Where Did I Want to Go?

I graduated high school in 2001. It was a strange year. Basically, I walked out of my high school and right into the local junior college in Jacksonville, Florida that fall. My first college class was on a Tuesday at 9am. It was a math class, and, to be honest, I was running a little late that day. As I walked across campus, I saw everyone running wildly and jumping into their cars. It was absolute chaos on my first day as a college student. I was escorted off the grounds by campus police and told to jump under a park bench and put my head down on my way out.

Moments later, I found out that a Boeing 757 had hit the World Trade Center, and it was unclear at the time whether or not our country was being invaded. After leaving campus that day, I was really sure about where I *didn't* want to go. I knew I wanted to do something better with my life. I knew I wanted to make a difference in the world. I was angry and hurt that day about what happened to my country, and I swore I was going to become wealthy. I wanted to achieve a high net worth, travel the world, and then give back most of my earnings to other people to help make the world a better place. I can thankfully say I am still on this path. For me, success is not just about earning a six-figure income, working short weeks, or finding time to work on my golf swing. It's more about spending quality time with my wife, Patricia, and our kids while earning enough disposable income to put into investment properties. With enough income and net worth, I can achieve all these goals every month and still have some money left over to donate to charitable funds and other causes that I care about.

So, to recap: Success for me personally is earning a consistent six-figure income, only working part time, and spending quality time with my family. It also means owning 25 single family homes free and clear, bringing in a healthy rental income, and then donating a large portion of my income to my preferred charitable organizations and causes. Your success and answer to the question of where you want to go may look very different from my own. It's up to you to do some soul searching to figure out exactly where you want to go and what success actually looks like for you.

How Much Time Did I Have to Reach My Destination?

Well, I guess if we want to get technical, I had 13 years to reach my destination. Once again, I really didn't have my life together back then, and I was too young to respect any success I had achieved. Early on, I blew most of the money I earned from real estate deals on cars, toys, traveling abroad, and partying with my friends. It wasn't until I matured in business and in life that I began to respect what I had and became motivated to develop a solid plan for success. Once I finally got it together, I was able to take stock of myself and discover the true meaning of Joe's early teachings.

So, fast-forward to today. As a full-time real estate entrepreneur and a family man, I am still working on my long-term goals for retirement, and to reach the full potential of my ultimate success plan. How long do I have to get there? Well, at the time of this writing, I have 30 years, 11 months, 20 days, and a few hours to get my 25 free and clear rental homes. As I work towards this goal, I will need to maintain my six-figure income and invest in my home life. I'll also want to spend some time helping to build churches and schools for struggling families in third-world countries. I believe it is very important that you have an extremely accurate idea of how long you have to reach your destination.

Once you have a strong grasp of your timeline, you can begin to snowball your successes by meeting small goals first. Maybe getting your real estate license is a goal you need to accomplish to motivate yourself and propel forward. Maybe paying off your mortgage is a goal you need to complete before purchasing your first rental property. Perhaps saving up 15 grand is a milestone you need to achieve to give you the courage to do your first fix-and-flip deal. Whatever your goals, you need to write them down now and map out how long you have to accomplish them.

Once you get your goals outlined and your timeline written down, you can begin to fill in the gaps by defining short-term goals. When you get really good at this, you will be able to define long-term goals twenty years out while maintaining short-term goals that are less than a year. By the time you quit your day job and jump into real estate investing full time, you will be mapping out your day-to-day goals while your bank account swells beyond your wildest dreams.

Now put down this book for a moment, grab a pen and paper, and take some serious stock of yourself. I can guarantee that if you don't take the time to run through this exercise, you'll just end up being that overconfident 17-year-old dreaming of his future success with no real plan to get there.

CHAPTER 2

Real Estate Wholesaling

A wholesaler locates good deals, negotiates a purchase price and terms, and then sells the deal to someone else. Some wholesalers never own the property, and some close on the property purchase before reselling it. Regardless of the exact mechanics of the deal, the concept is the same—buying and selling property in as-is condition.

I have a tremendous track record as a wholesaler, and it can be an exceptionally profitable business. However, running a thriving wholesaling operation requires a lot of expertise as well as some good, old-fashioned "hustle."

Unfortunately, the world abounds with gurus who will sell you information on becoming a "wholesaler." I have friends who have spent tens of thousands of dollars trying to learn the wholesaling business. The truth is, the term "wholesaling" has many different definitions. While many gurus teach their students how to scan everywhere, find deals, re-advertise them at a higher price, and then engineer a difficult closing to make a couple of thousand bucks, I teach my students to approach wholesaling as a *real business*. I prefer to teach you how to acquire a controlling interest, which then gives you the legal and ethical right to market the property.

Building a successful wholesaling business begins with building a customer base. Skip this important step (which can be done quickly) and you will always be hustling to find a buyer before your contract expires. To this day, I still wholesale deals, and most of them sell within a few hours of being emailed out to my customer list. Why waste your time "hustling deals" for a few thousand dollars when you can learn how to build a profitable wholesaling business that can provide a long-term, six-figure income?

One benefit of building and maintaining a wholesale customer base is that, even though your main business may evolve as ours has, you never want to pass up a good, profitable deal. Perhaps your cash is low or your rehab crews are too busy to take on another project. But don't pass it up! Instead, gain an equitable interest and flip it to one of your customers—someone who isn't as good at finding deals as you are.

Adam and I only buy properties that we are willing to keep in our own personal portfolios. And we only buy properties from two sources: individual owners and financial institutions. If we buy a property that we cannot sell quickly, we simply keep it in our rental portfolio. This has allowed us to build a reputation for closing on EVERY deal that we commit to. We insist on good value, a good property, and marketable title. Our customers have learned to expect the same from us, and we usually have more available buyers than properties to sell. I really believe that our philosophy of buying properties that we would want to keep ourselves is the main reason our wholesaling and investing operation has survived for over three decades.

Back in December of 2001, I made a decision to leave my six-figure project manager job to return to real estate investing. It was something I had done in the eighties, and one of my best friends had never left the business. His advice to me at the time was "keep your job!" Seems he was struggling to buy properties at workable prices. He told me the market was nothing like it had been back when I was operating as a full-time wholesaler and rehabber. His exact words were "you will never buy houses like you did back in the eighties."

Fortunately, his words were proven true. My best year in the eighties was around 30 house deals. In 2002, I turned 52 houses. My first order of business was to study every bit of updated investment education that I could get my hands on. I'm pretty good at absorbing, analyzing, and formatting information, and I soon had my business plan ready to implement. I based my acquisition strategy on buying from two sources: MLS properties and motivated sellers. I recruited a real estate agent to glean the MLS listings for suitable properties and to submit my offers, and I developed my own system for locating and reaching out to motivated sellers. The system is based on sending postcards and letters to non-owner occupants, offering to pay them cash for their houses. Although these buying tools have evolved and become more efficient over the years, we still use them to buy 90% of our houses.

Ever wonder why Bulldogs have flat noses? I believe it may come from "chasing parked cars." My marketing encourages sellers to call *me*. I don't look up owners of vacant houses and call them. I actually ignore for sale signs. When I initiate a call to a seller, I am at a distinct negotiating disadvantage, but when they call me, I enjoy the stronger position. All of our marketing is designed to get a seller to call us. To be effective, you need to understand the purpose of your advertising copy. Your purpose is *not* to buy houses and it is *not* to qualify prospects. The single purpose is *to get a property owner to call you.*

Now, if you have done proper research, you will have created a list of motivated sellers who own houses that you want to buy. Don't say anything in your advertising copy that does not help solicit a phone call.

I still personally answer every call from a motivated seller. Our business philosophy includes doing what we are best at ourselves and hiring others to do everything else. The first contact is critical.

You must be able to eliminate prospects that you have a low chance of buying from and move good prospects forward.

Once you have identified a prospect who you feel you can do business with, it is time to inspect the property. You will need to develop an understanding of renovation costs and calculate the after-repair value of the property. Next, you will need to determine your offer amount, make the offer, and negotiate your way to writing a purchase contract. Below you will find a few of my do's and don'ts of dealing with sellers.

DO...

1. Insist that the seller tell you how much they need from selling the property. If they won't do this, they are either fishing for a free appraisal or they're not far enough along in the selling decision for you to do business with them. Ask them if there is a mortgage or any liens or judgments on the property. If they inherited the home, is probate completed?
2. Check county records to gather basic information, such as: Do they own the property? When did they buy it and how much did they pay? Where does the property appraiser value the property? Did they get a warranty deed, quit-claim deed, or buy the property at a tax sale? A few minutes of investigation could save you a lot of time dealing with a non-owner, a bad title, or another deal-killing issue.
3. Make your purchase offer quickly (no more than 2 days) and convince the seller that you are a serious buyer who always closes the deal.
4. Follow through on your promises and expect your seller to do the same. Your purpose is to make friends with the owner and then convince your new friend to help you solve their problem by buying their property.

DON'T...

1. Waste time with "shaky" sellers as they will almost always back out before the deal closes.

2. Speak badly about or "dog" the property. The seller may have fond memories of the home. You can always find something nice to say about the property. My favorite comment is "I'll bet this was a really nice home in its day. When you sell it to me, it will undergo a full restoration and will become a nice home again." I can honestly say that about the most deteriorated and dirtiest of properties.

3. Try to buy from sellers who are not ready to sell. If the house is not a "problem," the seller is not yet motivated.

4. Begin marketing a property that you do not have a written contract to purchase. It is just bad practice and is actually illegal in most states.

Once you have a property under contract, you are ready to present it to your buyers list. If you have done your homework, you will know the retail value and/or expected rental income, the amount of repairs needed, and the cash profit or net income your buyer can expect to earn. We will cover all of these topics later in the book, but for now, let's talk about building your buyers list.

Building Your Buyers List

There are many types of buyers list. Some contain a massive number of "prospects," while others are more refined and contain a higher quality of "probable" buyers. While other wholesalers boast of a massive list containing thousands of buyers, we tend to lean toward a smaller and higher quality buyers list. We have had personal contact with the majority of the buyers on our list. Having been involved in investor education for many years, our list includes my students, existing and past customers, and prospects who have been guided to us by our internet marketing and/or social media outreach. You can build a list quickly with Google advertising, but it can be very expensive. In my opinion, providing education is absolutely the greatest list-building tool in existence.

One of the keys to my early wholesaling success was my desire to learn everything I could about real estate investing. I would study hard and pass on what I learned to my potential buyers. By providing free education, I was able to attract buyers and bring them to the point where they were ready to pull the trigger and buy my wholesale deals. I would do everything I could to ensure their success. After all, if they did not attain the results I touted, they would never become repeat customers, and I would have to find a new buyer for every deal. I remained a wholesaler for about three years. I began teaching my students about renovation, but the natural progression was to simply build a renovation company, and, later, for my son Adam to build a management company. Life was a lot simpler when I was a pure wholesaler, just not as profitable and certainly not as interesting or fulfilling.

Years ago, I was a member of a real estate investing club where we had a "deal of the month" competition. The prize was a nice, inscribed wall plaque. Each participant would come to the front of the group, describe their deal in detail, and then the audience would vote for what they saw as the best deal. On that day, there were three deals, and I was the last to present. Deals one and two were complicated deals with high profits. Each of them required lots of expertise; they were what I like to call "long-legged deals."

After hearing their level of expertise and profit, my little $3,000 deal didn't have a chance. I knew I couldn't out-profit them, so maybe I could out present them? I thought back to one of my favorite movies, *Jeremiah Johnson*. The following was my presentation...

In the movie, Robert Redford played the "rookie" mountain man, Jeremiah, and Will Geer the older, experienced mountaineer, Bear Claw. One day Bear Claw asks Jeremiah a simple question: "Can you skin Griz?" Jeremiah answered, "Of course I can skin a grizzly bear." The next scene occurs about a week later. Bear Claw is flying down the mountain with a 500-pound delirious grizzly bear snapping at his back. He is yelling for Jeremiah to open the front door. Jeremiah opens the cabin door and in comes old Bear Claw and the bear. As the old guy exits and slams the rear cabin door behind him, his parting words are "skin this and I'll go get you another one." I don't think I have ever seen a clearer illustration of the wholesaling business.

The "deal of the month" plaque still looks great on my office wall.

Consider Becoming a Real Estate Wholesaler

If you possess the required attributes and are willing to work hard, you can make a lot of money in the wholesaling business. I believe many people fail along this path because it is grossly oversold by the gurus. They tell you that all you need to do to become successful is to buy their $1,000 education package. Their next claim is always "anybody can do it."

Sure, anybody can get lucky and find a deal or two. If, however, you want to build a wholesaling operation that can provide strong, lasting income, then you need to learn to do it *right*. As with any real estate path, step one is to learn what you will need to be successful. Next, analyze your assets and abilities to determine if wholesaling is for you. Finally, you need to acquire REAL education that teaches you how to build a profitable and sustainable wholesaling business. The best source of this education is from someone who can not only document their long-term success, but is also still wholesaling property.

You can earn a very good living in the wholesaling business. For big-time success, you will need refined buying skills, renovation estimating expertise, good negotiating technique, above average marketing skills, and a lot of good, old-fashioned "hustle." Keep in mind, it will take time to develop into an effective wholesaler. Most successful wholesalers are very competitive people. A "laid-back" attitude won't be an asset in this business. A lot of gurus are teaching "virtual wholesaling," which I define as "fishing for newbie investor suckers." If you decide to pursue wholesaling, learn how to do it in a manner that benefits both you *and* your customers.

Adam's Take on Wholesaling

Joe and I run a real estate investor networking group with over 2,000 active investors in Florida. We hold networking events every month in Jacksonville, and it's a great chance to chat and network with other motivated individuals who love earning profits from real estate investing. Our attendees each possess a plethora of skills that differ from one another.

Each investor has a unique story and a different level of experience. Some have done a few deals and are ready to take things to the next level. Other investors have done deals for years and are looking for strategic partners and vendors. We also get a considerable number of newbie investors who have never done a deal and are looking to get their feet wet.

For some crazy reason, when we chat with the newbies, many of them tell us the same thing. They'll say that they don't have any money saved up to invest, but they attended a big event sponsored by one of the real estate investor gurus where they learned from an "expert" with a TV show that you don't actually need any money after all. We always ask them the same question: "How do you plan on accumulating wealth without your own money?" It's always the same answer. They tell us their plan is to start out as a wholesaler and earn tons of cash, and then after they have a high income, they will start buying up rental property, earn cash flow, and invest their money.

Now believe it or not, I am an extreme optimist when it comes to making a living as an entrepreneur. You've heard my story, and you know it's my biggest career passion. Still, with all that being said, I believe it is paramount to paint a realistic picture of what it's like being a wholesaler. To accurately depict the business, let me share a few real-life stories. I can give you my opinion all day long, but I think it will have a more lasting impact if I just tell you about a few investors I know who have chosen this path.

1. **Wholesaler #1**—No license. Estimated yearly earnings before taxes = $50-60K. Marginal reputation. Low skill. Low property knowledge. High sales. High productivity.
2. **Wholesaler #2**—Licensed real estate agent. Estimated yearly earnings before taxes = $70-80K. Too much overhead. Husband and wife both work full time as wholesalers. Bad reputation. Low property knowledge. High sales. High productivity. Mid skills.
3. **Wholesaler #3**—No license. Estimated yearly earnings before taxes = $20-30K. Low skill. Low property knowledge. No reputation. Low sales. Low productivity.
4. **Wholesaler #4**—Licensed real estate agent. Estimated yearly earnings before taxes = $120K. High skill. Mid property knowledge.

The reality of being a wholesaler is that it's extremely hard to make a full-time living at it. Most so-called wholesalers I meet have not even done their first deal. Many of the wholesalers who have done a few deals cannot actually get a company off the ground or make a living out of it. It's easy to stare at this list of wholesalers and dream about making it as one of them, but please just know that it's particularly hard to actually achieve high levels of success year after year. In fact, of the wholesalers I personally know, there's only a small handful that most of us in the biz would actually consider a huge success.

With all that being said, there are some great stories out there. People really do quit their day jobs and go into wholesaling and make a living from selling real estate investment properties. Let's take some time and talk about the most successful wholesalers out there. Why waste your time working your butt off to become an investor only to discover that you're barely bringing in enough dough each month to cover your basic living expenses?

As you can see from the real-life examples of wholesalers above, Wholesaler #4 beat them all in his yearly earnings. He is a highly skilled, licensed real estate agent with mid-level property knowledge. Let's dig deeper into who he is as a wholesaler and why he's more successful than the others. Please note that when I mention property knowledge, I am talking about how well our wholesaler knows the structural integrity of a property and how much real repair the property needs to get it rent ready or renovated to sell to a home buyer.

If I had to rate myself as a wholesaler, I would fall into category #4 as well. I am a licensed Florida real estate broker, with high marketing and business development skills. My actual knowledge of the physical aspects of properties is average or mid level. I grew up with a father who operated his own construction company and still does to this day. I have learned a lot about building and renovating single family properties over the years, and most of my knowledge comes from managing renovations on my own personal deals as well as using labor from Joe's construction company.

I worked for Joe for years before we actually became partners, and I learned a lot by shadowing him in the field and watching him manage renovations and run construction crews. If you plan on becoming a wholesaler who earns six figures, you need to learn some basic construction knowledge. It will give you a huge leg up on the competition. I would estimate that 95% of the wholesalers I've come across in this field have limited knowledge of what it will actually take to effectively fix up a property to rent or flip.

Many wholesalers are trying to make a quick buck and want nothing to do with telling you what it will truly take to repair the property. The ones who do go the extra mile and throw up an estimate of what it will take to fix the home are almost always wrong. They usually do not take the time to get a formal estimate from a contractor, either. This is partly because the numbers are usually higher than they would want them to be.

If the renovation numbers go up, then the deal becomes less attractive and therefore harder for the wholesaler to sell quickly. The problem with inaccurately estimating repairs on an investment property is you develop a reputation for providing bad deals. The investors you sell to end up spending more on fixing the property than they had originally expected, and they will not forget your error or dishonesty on the repair numbers. In their eyes, you killed their deal, and you are not going to get repeat sales or good referrals from these disgruntled buyers. Even if you unintentionally underestimated the repairs, word will eventually get around as your scorned buyers tell every investor they know about your unethical behavior. After a while, you will be unable to wholesale any more deals. In the end, you'll end up hanging your head, calling up your old boss, and begging them to give you back your previous desk job.

If you want to make it as a wholesaler, you need to figure out how to turn your job into a business. One of the reasons Joe and I have been able to turn our wholesaling operation into a full-fledged, turn-key real estate company is due to how we structured our part-nership in the beginning. As I said previously, Joe and I were not always partners. We were a small family company, and I earned my living from real estate commissions that I got from the bank foreclosure listings we purchased. At the time, I was in my twenties and doing pretty well for myself. I had no idea how much my dad was earning, but I knew it was *way* more than I was making. So I started to get more involved in doing actual deals, and I studied hard to try to develop a working business model to help me further my career and increase my yearly earnings. I strongly believed I could help the family do better than we'd been doing since the real estate bubble burst in 2007.

Eventually, I became an active real estate broker and founded my own company. This happened just before the real estate market crashed. Joe and I agreed that a collaboration between a general contractor and a real estate broker was a perfect partnership. I would handle the paperwork, contracts, negotiations, closings, marketing for buyers and sellers, and all the aspects of managing the "real estate business" side of our company. I would complete all these tasks through my real estate brokerage. I am a licensed REALTOR®, and I have to adhere to the Florida Real Estate Commission and the ethics that bind me to my license. I am obligated to treat the public with the professional standards that have been agreed upon by all licensed REALTORS® through our code of ethics. I have intimate relationships with many other real estate agents, bank employees, and respected business professionals in my community. You can usually find me in a business park meeting with clients over good food in nice neighborhoods wearing business professional clothing.

Joe is the complete opposite. He usually shows up wearing blue jeans and a hoodie. Sometimes he's in flip flops with a raccoon-eye sunburn from his previous morning of fishing. He works hard in the field spending quality time at the actual properties estimating repairs and organizing our renovations. He dislikes paperwork and reserves one day per week for his construction company billing and any other office work he needs to do. He loves solving problems and finding new ways to make floor plans flow better, cabinets fit into small spaces more effectively, and finding the sweet spot on quality versus speed with his renovation crews. Joe is our contractor, and he handles all of the physical aspects of our real estate investor business with his turn-key construction company.

Joe and I believe we have found the perfect partnership to earn money as a real estate wholesaler. I can tell you that since we paired up, each of us has been able to earn a six-figure net income every year for more than seven years. You may decide that staying away from estimating repairs and not taking a partner is the path for you. While it does mean you won't have to split your profits, you may also find that you actually end up working harder. I do have to tell you that Wholesaler #4 from our list above already had a decade of experience under his belt before he was able to bring in those six figures. Of course, he wasn't fortunate enough to have mentors helping him along the way. So if you work hard and follow this model for success, you can do very well as a real estate investment wholesaler.

Still, I would caution you that if you do decide to take on a contractor partner, and you get good at running a wholesale business together, you might end up leaving behind the wholesaler path altogether and founding your own turn-key real estate company. Ultimately, it's all up to you. Your experiences will likely be different than Joe's and mine have been. With enough knowledge and passionate hustle, you can become very successful at getting good deals under contract and then reselling those contracts for quick cash!

Good luck out there, and if you wouldn't mind, please send our turn-key real estate investment company some good deals so we can sell them to our clients for high net profits. Our clients won't mind either; they'll be too busy stuffing their pockets with all the positive cash flow they've earned each month from the rental properties we sold them.

CHAPTER 3

Fixing & Flipping Houses

Fix and flip, also known as "retailing," is very popular among new investors. There are multiple television shows depicting the fix and flip process. Most of these shows depict the process fairly accurately. Few of them, however, show the complete financial transaction.

I have noticed that items such as insurance, utility costs, lending costs, sales commissions, and other costs are often ignored. What sounds like a great profit may not be so good after a real, final accounting. However, when done properly, fixing and flipping houses can be very profitable. If, like me, you derive pleasure from rebuilding and improving things, you might enjoy fixing up a house and flipping it to a retail buyer. Other positive factors include the fact that you are helping families by providing good housing and improving neighborhoods.

Here in Jacksonville, Florida, the "sweet spot" for retailing seems to be around the $175,000-$250,000 range. As of this writing, in early 2017, mortgage rates are low and sales in this price range are brisk. This price range represents our middle class buyers. These buyers have adequate income and credit to qualify for good financing. The fix-and-flip process includes funding the project, locating and acquiring a distressed property, renovating, marketing, and closing the resale. Expect to work closely with real estate acquisition agents, renovation contractors, and real estate listing agents.

Like every other path, fix and flip has its negatives. First and

foremost, it's a "job," and like any other job, when you quit working, your income stops. I have counseled many students who, after
doing an accurate estimate of their probable income from fixing
and flipping, decided to keep their regular job and pursue another
path in the real estate investor business. Another negative is that
the retail market is tied closely to interest rates and the availability
of financing. When rates rise, your business will slow. You should
do quite well when rates are low; however, low rates draw other
"flippers" into the market, increasing competition, and making it
more difficult to find good deals on distressed houses.

I do not recommend borrowing hard money to do retail deals.
The "interest only" rates are too expensive, and by the time you
purchase the property and then fix it up, you will have to bear high
monthly payments from the time of acquisition until the final sale of
the house. The average fix-and-flip project will take you six months
from start to finish, and the hard money will eat up a large portion
of your profits. By the time you calculate your true final profit when
using hard money, you will discover that you have just done a lot of
hard work for a minimal net return.

If you want to fix and flip, use your own money or find a private
funding partner who you can split the profits with. This partner
should not be a company that provides loans to investors, but an
individual with their own liquid cash who is willing to partner with
you and do the deal. You find, organize, and manage the deal, and
your investor partner puts up the money. When the house is sold,
you will split the net proceeds at a pre-negotiated ratio (50/50 is
common).

I have done many retail flip deals this way in the past, and they
have worked out well. One important detail of a successful partnership is a clear delineation of responsibilities. I make sure my
partners understand that I am the expert and make all decisions;

they are along for the ride and to make money. My responsibility to them is 100% related to funding—not acquisition, renovation, or final sale of the property.

My fix-and-flip activity during the past several years is probably only around 50 houses or so. The mix includes both rehabbed and new construction homes. While I have enjoyed a few notable successes, I have also suffered from retailing failures, most notable in 2007 when the retail mortgage market literally imploded. I was left holding several new construction homes that were secured by construction loans. It took me several years to fully recover from those losses, but I learned a few very valuable lessons—namely that leverage that works *for you*, can also work *against you*. I also learned that Florida real estate actually *can* decline in value.

With that said, I have done a few very profitable fix-and-flip deals. We bought a distressed home in Springfield (one of Jacksonville, Florida's historic districts) for $35,000 cash. After $100,000 in improvements, we sold it for $210,000. Even after paying all commissions and soft costs, our net profit exceeded $45,000. Another profitable home was one that I purchased for only $6,000, repaired for $35,000, and then resold for $65,000.

I have not personally flipped a house to an owner-occupant in over two years. The closer I get to retirement, the more I need to concentrate on creating passive income instead of a quick profit. I do have a close friend who is one of the more successful retailers in the area. He works with investors to fund his deals, does high-quality renovations, and retails for top dollar. His most successful deals are in the $175,000 to $300,000 market, and he only operates in the best-selling neighborhoods. He is constantly complaining that he has to pay too much for properties, and he cannot seem to keep a quality renovation contractor. However, he must be making money as he keeps on buying, rehabbing, and selling retail properties.

If you want to fix and flip, you need to buy only in desirable and fast-selling neighborhoods, do beautiful renovations, stage the home, and choose a real estate agent to market your finished product. Time is of the utmost importance as the retail market is subject to rapid changes. In the beginning, I would suggest passing on houses that need major renovations and concentrating on homes that only need cosmetic repairs. While your profit may be lower, your turnaround time should be much less, resulting in less exposure and risk due to market changes.

Consider Becoming a Fix-and-Flip Retailer

If you need extra income, or even a new career, and you have (or can obtain) at least $100,000 cash, you might want to begin as a fix-and-flip retailer.

If you begin with fix and flip, don't underestimate the financial risk or the amount of time retailing can consume. The critical path for new investors is often getting the renovation done on time and on budget. The risk will be lower if you have cash and can avoid leveraging. As of this writing, fixing and flipping is the favored business plan among new investors.

Currently, interest rates are low and nice homes are selling quickly. There are, however, a lot of investors in the fix-and-flip business. Many are new to the business and simply pay too much for the as-is property. Unfortunately, these uneducated buyers run up the price for distressed properties and increase the competition. Still, if you can buy a profitable home in a good neighborhood, resale should be good. I personally don't do a lot of fixing and flipping as it is tied closely to interest rates, and conditions for retailing depend on a lot of external factors that can change quickly. At this point in my investing career (nearing retirement), I am not willing to tolerate very much risk.

As I mentioned earlier, one of my best friends is a very successful retailer. He has dedicated a lot of time and effort to learning his craft and has also retained his full-time career. If you decide to follow this path, just be wary of borrowing from institutional lenders, and do it right. Buy in good, fast-selling neighborhoods and do top-quality renovations and staging. Last but not least, hire the best professional real estate agent in the area to market your renovated homes.

Adam's Take on Fix and Flips

Fix and flipping is the stuff of dreams. Turn on the fix-and-flip shows, grab a cup of coffee, and sharpen your design skills, right? We all dream about buying that ugly property in the neighborhood and fixing it up. You know the one I'm talking about—it hasn't been painted in 15 years, the shutters are nearly falling off their hinges, and the color schemes on the inside are horrible. If we could just get inside and peel off that horrible wood paneling from the 1970s, we could make it a beautiful home to live in again. We're convinced that if we could just buy it, fix it up, and modernize the property, we'd rake in $20-30K—heck, maybe even $50K!

But when's the last time your best investment earned you a 110% return?

The reality of doing fix and flips, or retailing as we have called it, is that the process can take far longer than you realize, and the average net return can be far less than you anticipate.

To begin, you will need to purchase the property for 50% of its value, or 50 cents on the dollar. This means that if the property is going to be worth $200K after you repair it, you will need to purchase the property as-is for only $100K. You may be wondering, "Why so cheap, Adam? That's not as cheap as I saw on that glamorous rehabber show last night." Well, here's the truth: Those shows are not being entirely honest with you. Now, I am not saying they are conspiring to deceive you or anything. However, what I am saying is that the goal of rehabber TV shows has nothing to do with showing you how to do profitable deals.

The producer's goal is to get you to watch the show. In truth, the producers have no idea what a good deal is, and they are just generalizing the numbers and taking the word of the reality TV stars on whether or not the deal on the show is actually a good one.

Would you like to know how I figured this out? Well, for starters, I can run the numbers by seeing what they paid for the home, how much they spent on renovations, and then what they sold the home for. I know what the average holding and sales costs are from doing so many deals in the past and working with title companies and real estate agents. I also know these shows tend to give you gross profit projections and rarely share the *actual net numbers*. These hidden expenses that no one ever seems to mention eat directly into your bottom line and will make most of the deals you see on these shows not actually worth doing. I have also had the opportunity to speak closely with the producers who work with these big media powerhouses—the ones who organize and produce real estate investor TV shows about ordinary people who fix and flip homes for profit.

Joe and I have been approached numerous times over the last couple of years about doing our own fix-and-flip show. We spent a lot of time interviewing with producers and chatting back and forth about what the show would be about, and what it would be like to watch ourselves do deals on the big screen. So, I can tell you this with certainty: They could care less about the deals you are doing. They really only care about whether or not the viewers will mesh with your character, what you will look like on camera, whether you possess an interesting personality, and things like that—all the fun stuff that makes us an exciting character that people want to watch. This is what they're really looking for. So, if you are willing to channel your inner Tim "The Tool Man" Taylor, and if you can fake like you consistently conduct profitable deals, then you might be a good fit for your own fix-and-flip TV show.

However, Joe and I couldn't get away from focusing on doing the actual deals and getting excited about making money. We have most of our operation pretty well groomed, so I guess it would have been boring to just watch us sitting on our laptops, making casual phone calls to our highly trained team.

By now you may be a little bummed out thinking we killed your dream. Well, we're sorry about that, but there's an important lesson here. You need to know what fixing and flipping is really like out there in the real estate market. Joe and I meet new investors every month who are always telling us they want to earn some quick cash by fixing and flipping on the side. This typical investor wants to keep his or her day job and earn some easy money in their spare time by doing the fix and flip thing they saw on the plasma screen last night. Sounds a lot like a hobby now, doesn't it? Well, it can be.

However, the only way to *consistently* earn healthy net returns on fix-and-flip deals is to make it a *business*. Now, just like any other business, you are going to have to figure out how to decrease your expenses and increase your sales. You are going to have to start making connections, building a vendor list, becoming a master marketer, and all those other skills needed to buy houses cheap, fix them up, and resell them to home buyers.

But your first step to success as a fix-and-flip rock star should be to build your dream team.

What Your Dream Team Should Look Like

You're going to need to enlist the help of several professionals if you want to run a successful fix-and-flip operation. Let's take a closer look at who these people are and why you need them.

1. **Buyer's Real Estate Agent.** You will need a licensed and experienced real estate agent to work the buying side. This agent will be skilled in filtering MLS listings every day, loading up a spreadsheet with possible deals, getting you inside the properties, writing contracts, and working closings. They need to be able to relate well with all members of the team and help everyone keep a tight watch on bank inventory and what current prices are doing in the real estate market.

2. **Seller's Real Estate Agent/Bank Listing Agents.** You or your buyer's agent will need to make contact and create strong relationships with all the bank listing and seller agents in your local marketplace. Many of the best fix-and-flip deals will come from the banks. The market for buying bank foreclosures is extremely competitive, so you will need the help of the seller's real estate agent to get any quality inventory.

   If you want to become known as a quality buyer in your local marketplace, you need to pay cash, close in less than 30 days, and never back out of a deal. Once you get a solid reputation with many of the banks' real estate agents, you can get preference from asset managers who know you will close on the deal. If you do have a dedicated buying agent, then they will need to develop the same relationships with all the bank agents. If you back out of deals more than once with any of the major banks, HUD, or Fannie Mae, you can easily get blacklisted, and they will no longer allow you to buy their properties. Reputation is everything in the banking industry, so you'd better tread lightly.

3. **Wholesalers.** When the bank inventory dries up, or you

can't seem to find profitable fix-and-flip deals, then whole-salers are your best bet. They spend all day long digging up deals, and they usually have a few or know of someone else who does. They will want to be paid as a middleman, of course, but you really shouldn't care if they earn a healthy profit as long as you do too. You need some inventory and they have some good deals. Once you get through a few closings together, they will call you first when a good deal comes in that they know will work for you.

Keep in mind that you will need to train them a little bit on what you consider a good deal and what you're will-ing to buy. It's true that they will sometimes send you junk deals as well, so you need to be good at saying no without souring the relationship. If you act professional and can successfully build a healthy relationship with them, they will send you deals all the time. Once you get a dozen wholesalers all working for you, the deals will come in like magic!

4. **Contractor.** One of the most important members of your team will be your contractor. They can be a general con-tractor who knows how to build anything or a residential contractor who just focuses on homes. I have found that the best contractors will be the ones who have not only built new homes, but have renovated homes as well. Be-lieve it or not, it can actually be more difficult to stay within budget when working on a large renovation than it is to just build a new home from scratch.

When you're building new, many of the costs can be easily tied down by getting estimates from subcontrac-tors on what the work will cost. If the contractor wants to know what it will cost to pour the slab, he just calls up the foundation guy and gets a quote. If he wants to find out what it will take to install the plumbing, he just calls that subcontractor and gets his quote. Everything is different with a renovation. The contractor will have to search for handymen to do most of the work that does not require a permit. He'll also need to have a firm grasp of what it costs to handle small projects and what material and labor costs will be. The costs can vary drastically, and he can really screw you over if he doesn't have experience in running renovation projects.

You will need to run on a lean budget to turn a profit with a fix-and-flip deal, so you really need to search for the right contractor if you want to be successful. Many fix and flippers will actually partner up with their contractor. If you cut him in on a portion of the profit, he will really work hard for you. If you want to make it in the long run and earn a living from fix and flip, you will almost certainly have to cut your contractor in as a partner. The beauty of this strategy is that once he's a partner, you can get your contractor to view and estimate repairs on all the deals you buy before you put them under contract.

5. **Home Inspector.** During the first 10 days of the contract on a typical transaction, you will be able to inspect the property. You need to develop a relationship with a reputable home inspector who can view the property and make sure you do not have any major structural issues. Your inspector can also provide a detailed report on what repairs need to be done. Be very careful here, though. Please remember that home inspectors are not always contractors. They can provide a separate opinion and will normally do so for just a few hundred dollars, but they are usually not

qualified enough to provide a full scope of work. They will give you a report in just a few days that you can use to begin to determine the current condition of the property. You will still need to bring in your contractor to sign off on any repairs that need to be done.

6. **Private Lender (if needed).** If you have your own cash, you can move on to #7. However, if you don't, you will need cash to purchase good deals at a discount. This is where a private lender comes in. The money isn't cheap, but you may consider partnering up with a lender to do the deal. I would plan on needing the money for six months. That's three months to get the property fixed up and three months to get to the closing table. I am assuming you are pricing the property to sell and can get a contract from a home buyer in the first 30 days.

7. **Staging Expert.** You can either hire a professional home stager or learn how to do it yourself. They will make your vacant home look attractive and lived in by adding furniture, decorations, and more. They will maximize square feet by strategically placing couches and side tables in the perfect locations to increase traffic flow. They will hang pretty paintings and choose just the right colors to draw the correct emotion from the viewing home buyers. Home buyers are very emotional when purchasing their dream home, and you really need to nail the presentation to ensure you can sell your fix and flip quickly.

8. **Marketing/Business Expert.** If you want to make a business out of fixing and flipping homes, you are going to need some marketing and business skills. Everything from branding your logo to designing your company website will come into play. You can either hire a marketing expert

to be part of your team or you can bring in a consultant to help you get set up.

9. **Title Company/Closing Attorney.** Having a good title agent or closing attorney to perform a proper title search will make or break you. We have put really good deals under contract for less than 50% of value, only to discover after running the title that there were a myriad of title issues that prevented the flip sale. You have to think about the fact that your end buyer will be a homeowner who obtains a conventional or governmental home loan. The institution they borrow the funds from is not going to issue the loan unless the seller can provide a clean and marketable title.

   A skilled closing attorney can identify and even fix bad title issues early in the closing process. Some of the best buys you will find have a bad title. You can create tons of value upfront by digging up bad title deals, fixing the title, and then renovating the property to sell as a flip. This of course is another strategy, but having a good title representative behind your transactions will increase your closing rate on fix and flips and open up your business to new profit ventures that you weren't even aware of.

10. **Mentor.** We saved the best for last. The most important member of your team is a qualified mentor to help you along the way. This should actually be the first member of your team. Before you pick up the phone and start touring properties with your local real estate agent, you should find a qualified mentor to help you analyze your strengths and weaknesses and what resources you have to work with.

   You will find it best to search for and seek out mentors

who have actually done tons of deals and have worked with students in the past. Joe and I are professional real estate investor mentors. We have personally coached, trained, and consulted for over 1,000 of our past students. Some of them went on to become very successful and now compete with us to do deals. Some of them got the training and never even did a deal. Many of them have done deals with us and continue to partner with us on deals to this day. I hope you will consider us in your search for a mentor, but if not, that's ok too. Just please be careful out there and choose someone who you feel will be a good fit for you personally. A good mentor will do a great job teaching you the ropes and enhancing your chances for future success.

The Non-Profitable Way to Do aFix-and-Flip Retail Deal

I spoke to a sophisticated business owner last week who just finished his first fix-and-flip deal. His wife helped decorate the home after learning how to pick mood colors and furniture that appealed to home buyers. They bought a beat-up bank foreclosure and made it beautiful. I asked him how the deal turned out. Did he make any money? Would he do it again? His simple answer was this: "I had a bunch of fun doing the deal, and we learned a lot throughout the process, but I already have a day job, and it earns a whole lot more than this one." In the end, they spent half a year on the project and only took home $10K on the deal. They put in more than 300 hours of their personal time over six months and were happy to get out of the deal alive.

The lesson? When doing these deals, you really need to consider what your time is worth. Are you willing to take the risks of owning a home and betting against the market to earn $10K in six months? In this couple's story, they had their own cash reserves but decided it wasn't worth the time and energy they'd invested. Now, imagine they had a 15% interest-only, hard-money loan (which is the going rate on the streets), and you can see how this would not have been a viable deal for the average person. It's really easy to lose money on a deal like this if you don't know what you are doing. There are many moving parts to the transaction, and you need to carefully monitor your time and energy to ensure you are actually earning money.

The Profitable Way to Do a Fix-and-Flip Retail Deal

I know of an investor who does fix and flips all the time in my hometown of Jacksonville, Florida. He happens to be one of our past students. We mentored him through his first three deals, and after that he went out on his own. Our mentoring included teaching him how to target a certain area where homes sell quickly, estimate repairs on the spot, submit offers to banks and auction websites efficiently, partner with lenders, complete high-quality retail renovations, market the property for resale, negotiate with home buyers, navigate inspections and appraisals, get to the closing table quickly, and, ultimately, to get his profit at the end of the deal. We even taught him how to set up his own business and how to properly structure his organization to reduce his tax burden and increase profits.

Today, he won't even view a property unless it's 50% of value or less. He has become very good at estimating the after-repair value, and he knows what homes sell for in the neighborhoods that he does deals in. He has been able to streamline his process by honing in on a couple of neighborhoods that he calls his "farms." If he does a marketing campaign to buy houses, he will flood his farm with as many offers to buy houses as he can. He hangs out in these areas all the time, and he meets neighbors and knocks on doors. This guy is willing to do the things that no one else wants to do. He digs up good deals and he often makes money when he buys.

He has also gotten very good with his renovations. His wife got involved some time ago and decided she would get a certificate for interior design at the local junior college. She watches HGTV every night and she knows what is hot and what is not with interior design. She also decided to get her own real estate license so they could save 3% on the listing side. He handles everything on the "dirty" side, including digging up ugly houses, running subcontractors during the renovation, and buying materials. She handles everything on the "clean" side, including staging the property, photographing it for the listing, creating websites to sell the property, and writing sales contracts with buyers. They do actually partner with a lender, but since they buy the properties for so cheap, they can afford the lending partner.

What makes them so successful is they have followed our system for finding good deals, renovating them quickly, and then pricing them to sell. The reason the other couple failed is they paid too much for the property in the beginning, the renovation took too long and went over budget, and they were forced to ask 105% of market value for the property. The Locklear-mentored couple was able to offer their very nice home for sale at 95% of market value. The crazy thing is, since they priced it below market, they got multiple bids and the price was driven up to 102% of market value. It sold in the first three days, and because they were their own seller's agent, they hustled to get to the closing table by controlling the closing process in-house. They earned $22K on their first deal, and it only took them 92 days from start to finish. Now, that's worth doing in your spare time!

Before they got into doing fix and flips, our mentee's wife was a stay-at-home mom who kept getting sucked into pyramid schemes to sell makeup. These days, she sells investment properties and her husband manages the renovations after-hours and on weekends.

Their yearly income has doubled, and they travel abroad often with their kids.

There is a profitable way to retail fix and flips, but you will need a solid system to follow and a mentor to save you time. If you skip these two important steps, it will cost you countless hours, and you'll end up paying with your blood, sweat, and tears. If you go this route, you will quickly fall into the School of Hard Knocks, just as Joe and I once did.

CHAPTER 4

Becoming a Lender and Understanding How to Borrow

I am going to reverse the order and tell you the negative first as there is only one drawback to becoming a lender that I know of: You need cash, and you need to be able to tie up that cash for anywhere from one to ten or more years. If you have the cash and can afford to let it ride for a few years, becoming a lender may be for you. Of course, there is also risk, which I'll talk about in a moment. But if you lend wisely, your risk of not getting repaid can mostly be avoided.

As a rule, I never borrow from brokers or banks, but I do business with several private lenders. Many of these lenders have done multiple deals with me as I recruited and educated most of them. They consistently earn 8-13% interest on their money. Some of them lend from their private savings accounts and some from self-directed IRAs.

The positive aspect of private lending includes great passive income that can be obtained with a minimum of time and effort. One word of caution, however: **You must become educated before lending money**. When done properly, lending can be one of the safest and most consistently profitable real estate investing paths. I have, however, heard scores of testimonies from lenders who lost money, and it's almost always due to the same problem. The problem is usually due to an inexperienced lender trusting someone, then later discovering that the borrower or partner who claimed to be an expert was just as inexperienced as the lender themself. If you have the cash, by all means, go for the 8-13% returns; just make sure to get an education first. You need to learn what you are doing before you fork over boatloads of cash to someone who lacks the proper experience to repay the money you lent them.

Before 2007, when mortgages were readily available and the market was solid, I sold a lot of turn-key houses to buyers who would ultimately refinance and hold the property for rental income. Fannie Mae, however, would require one year of ownership before allowing a cash-out refinance. Even if you paid cash for the property and came out-of-pocket for the repairs, getting your money back was still classified as a cash-out. To get around this seasoning issue, we discovered that if you were paying off an existing loan, the cash-out restriction did not apply. I actually had customers with cash on hand who preferred to borrow money to purchase and renovate a rental property. This allowed them to refinance as soon as the rehab was complete and move on to the next property. They would only spend their own cash once all available mortgages were acquired.

This provided a fantastic opportunity for private lending. I hooked up with a couple of local lenders who issued small loans in the $50,000 range. They charged up to 3 points and 15% interest. The loans were short term, so the borrowers cared little about how high the interest was. It was just the cost of doing business and getting as many Fannie Mae loans as possible.

From the lender's perspective, they had borrowers with great credit and adequate assets to prevent them from ever considering a default. This is the safest and most lucrative lending business that I know of. My lenders were not loan companies but simply individuals with cash who wanted to make good interest on their cash. That market is not as hot as it was before the mortgage crisis, but it does in fact still exist, and it can be a very safe and profitable strategy to earn high interest on your money.

Another market that is not as secure but is still profitable is lending money to fix and flippers to purchase and remodel their houses. When they close the flip sale, you are paid off. Your returns on this type of lending should average 13-15%, but let's look at some simple math. You will seldom have all of your available cash out in loans. If you have 1 million dollars available, you would need to work hard to have 75% of your capital working at any given point in time. This effectively reduces your returns by 25%, so a 15% interest rate becomes an actual 11.25% return on available cash.

If you are willing to educate yourself, private lending can be a safe and profitable business. Go in blind, however, and you will likely lose big money. I recently met a fellow at a business networking event who had inherited about $500,000. He had attended a seminar on private lending and was announcing to the attendees that he had money available to lend. Response was great, but he had no idea what he was doing.

Having no doubt that he would quickly lose his inheritance, I invited him to a class on private financing that I was teaching the following weekend. The class opened his eyes to how little he knew. We had breakfast later that week, and he ultimately decided to put his lending operation on hold.

Most of my current buyers are cash buyers, so I don't have a big demand for private funds. However, I do work with private lenders to provide mid-term financing for expansion of our family's private real estate rental portfolio. While we may never do business with each other, I will gladly help my new friend approach the market with wisdom and in a direction that will provide good returns with minimal risk. Now, let's take a look at some of the do's and don'ts of private lending.

DO...

1. Lend exclusively to experienced investors or new investors working under close mentorship with a proven, successful entrepreneur. When considering a loan, understand that most investors don't fail because they bought a bad deal. Most fail by exceeding the rehab budget, both in dollars and in time. Renovation and marketing experience are absolutely essential.

2. Find a good attorney or title company and stick with them. Only close loans with the company that will put your interest foremost. Insist on title insurance without non-standard exceptions.

3. Only lend with a first mortgage as security, never a second or lower mortgage.

4. Have the borrower provide an assignment of rents and property insurance, naming you as the lender and first payee.

5. Always place renovation repair funds in an escrow account that you control, and only release funds based upon work that has already been completed. Do NOT ever, and I mean ever, release funds to pay for work that has not already been completed.

6. If you are not familiar with checking renovation progress and quality, hire a professional to inspect for each repair draw. You can often pass on this cost to the borrower. Remember that the finished product will be your collateral.

DON'T...

1. Lend money to your close friends or relatives. My personal rule is that if my close friends or family need money and I have it available, I will consider a gift, but not a loan.

2. Let your personal feelings sway your lending decisions.

Lending is a business and you need to be consistent in your practices.

3. Exceed 70% loan-to-value (LTV), and always require the borrower to have some of their own money at risk in the deal.
4. Bend your rules just to get money out into the market.
5. Borrow money to loan to others. This is very dangerous.

Private lending can be very profitable, and when done properly, it can be very safe. Breaking the basic rules, however, can cost you a lot of money. This business is not very forgiving.

Consider Becoming a Real Estate Lender

If you have a lot of cash but a very limited amount of time, you should consider becoming a private lender for real estate deals. Without proper education, however, you can easily lose a ton of money or end up with junk properties if you are forced to take back a property. Once you learn the basics, lending is one of the safest real estate paths. However, if you are the type of person who likes to track every detail of your investment's progress and you need to be hands-on, lending is not for you.

If you are a results-oriented person and prefer to let others make the everyday decisions, you should be comfortable as a lender. The safest way to become a lender is to find an experienced and reputable fix and flipper or turn-key provider and begin lending to them. You need to escrow renovation repair funding and release money only after the work has been completed. Make sure title is good and you have an assignment of rents, insurance, and a valid first mortgage. A reputable attorney or title company that is experienced in dealing with real estate investors is vital to your safety and ultimate success as a lender.

Adam's Take on Lending

My ultimate goal is to get to the point in my life where I can lend large amounts of cash for profitable investment deals. I strongly believe that, in order to accumulate great wealth, you need to eventually fire your bank and then become the bank yourself! Sounds crazy, right? It's not.

You can attain immense amounts of wealth from lending money to investors who want to do deals. You do, however, need to understand each deal and the physical aspects of the property you are lending against. Although we would like to assume that all the deals we've lent money to will work out—and that we'll be repaid during the agreed upon loan period—the truth is, as a lender, you will have to take back a few properties from time to time. So, you need to be prepared to own the properties you lend against, just in case you end up taking the property back or calling the note due.

When I think of private lending, I always reflect back to the first private-money lender I borrowed from. Mr. Daniels was a savvy lender. He had guts, too. I can remember the first time I saw him roll up in his late-model Lincoln Town Car. We met him at a run-down junker of a house smack dab in the middle of the worst part of the ghetto. This had to be one of the shabbiest houses I had ever laid my eyes upon. It was crooked to begin with, and it looked like the floor was made of sandpaper. The house had no front yard, and I swear you could have rung the doorbell from the passenger seat of your car as you drove by. And you probably would have wanted to, as I'm quite sure we needed bulletproof vests just to get out of the car that day.

As it turned out, Mr. Daniels had just taken this property back from a borrower he had lent to. The borrower had failed to fix up the property as agreed and instead had rented out the junk property to drug users for a few years. Eventually, he jumped ship and stopped making his mortgage payment. But, instead of dragging out a nasty foreclosure proceeding and spending the $5-7K it would have cost him, Mr. Daniels talked the borrower into just giving the property back to him with no questions asked.

Joe and I had met Mr. Daniels at our local real estate investors association, and we saw some value in helping him out. We knew he was a wealthy individual, and if we could get him out of his current predicament, we stood a great chance of getting him to lend on our own future deals. So, we helped him get out of that property and into some great deals. Had he found us instead of that shady borrower, we would have fit him right into our program of doing profitable deals and escrowing the repair funds, which would've given him the right to inspect the work each week—all while paying back his loan in a reasonable amount of time.

Soon thereafter, Mr. Daniels did get plugged into our system and earned a ton of profit from lending to us. He was able to keep his money on the streets while getting into good deals on a regular basis. He earned 3 points on every loan he committed to, and I noticed that he preferred to loan the funds, earn the points, and then get his money back quickly. Once he got his money back, he wanted to do it again and again. I think he felt safe getting his money back every 30-60 days, and with the high return on his funds, he knew it was a worthy system to be part of.

Eventually, after years of working with Joe, I started doing deals with Mr. Daniels on my own. I wanted to purchase my first house to live in, and I found an amazing deal that was a bank foreclosure. The problem was the house was an absolute bomb, and I couldn't get any conventional lender to lend on a property that needed so much work. It wouldn't pass a home inspection and pretty much needed all the major components replaced.

I knew we had borrowed millions from Mr. Daniels over the

course of a few years, and I had built a direct relationship with him. I presented the deal to him, and he ended up lending me $90K cash to purchase the house, plus $30K in repair money. My wife, Patricia, and I were newlyweds, and we wanted to make a nest for our future kids. We ended up running $5K over our renovation budget, but the home was a showcase. We had burned through our personal savings, but Mr. Daniels had faith in us and lent us the additional $5K needed to finish paying the contractor.

After the home was renovated, we strolled down to our local credit union and refinanced the loan—paying off Mr. Daniel's hard-money loan. We ended up with a 78% loan-to-value (LTV) on a 30-year fixed mortgage at 4.5% interest. We were able to skip the private mortgage insurance due to getting in under 80% LTV. We lived in that house for six years and eventually sold it for $245K. Our net profit was around $100K. It was a win-win for us and our lender, and everyone was happy with the outcome.

Be Very Careful When Borrowing with Hard-Money Loans

Hard-money loans are just like they sound. They are easy to get, but hard on the borrower. Hard-money lenders will typically charge you 15% on an interest-only loan with 3 points paid upfront. If you consider a $200K loan needed to fund the purchase and renovations of a potentially profitable fix-and-flip deal, the payments can get steep quickly. At $200K, your mortgage payment will be $2,500 per month, and you will pay the lender $6,000 upfront.

I see real estate investors in the market all the time who are talking up fix-and-flip deals that they are offering as-is for 70% of value. So, let's use the numbers from above and analyze a typical fix-and-flip deal with a hard-money loan. Please keep in mind these numbers are coming from a typical deal in Jacksonville, Florida during our current real estate market. If you are analyzing deals in a more expensive market, just adjust the sales price and you'll get the same answer.

Hard-Money Loan Fix-and-Flip Example

Purchase Price at 70% of value - $200,000

After-Repair Value (Appraisal Value) - $285,000

Renovation Amount - $35,000

Hard-Money Cost at 6-Month's Interest - $23,625

Cost of Sale (6% Real Estate Agent's Commission + 2% of Closing Costs) - $22,800

Projected Net Profit = **$3,575**

I am sure when this investor first presented this deal, it sounded something like the advertisement below:

> *Fix and Flip Deal of the Month*
> *Attractive 3 bedroom and 2 bath brick home in an*
> *up-and-coming area. This is your chance to fix up*
> *a distressed property and make it gorgeous again*
> *while raking in a strong profit.*
> *Offered at only $200K*
> *After repair-value is $285K*
> *Needs $35K in repairs*
> *Financing Available*

Many new investors will see an advertisement like this and think they can easily earn $50K in profit. Even if they are quite smart and a bit skeptical, they'll often say to themselves, "Even if I only earn half of the projected $50K profit, I'll still be okay." By failing to analyze this type of deal correctly, these newbie investors will spend a lot of time only to find out that doing this type of deal was a waste of time.

So, where did they go wrong? Well, to start with, many investors who advertise deals for sale will misrepresent the repair amount. It's very important when you do a deal that you get an accurate estimate on what the repair amount will be. We will talk more about how to get an accurate estimate of repairs in future chapters, but for now, I want you to focus on the hard money aspect of this fix-and-flip advertisement. Do you see how they just snuck it right into the ad?

Many investors will see this ad and just do some simple math. They will run their numbers for profit just like they are back in 3rd grade and learning simple arithmetic.

Let's take a look at a normal person's analysis of a deal like this:

After-Repair Value (ARV): $285,000
Less Purchase Price: -200,000
Less Repairs: -35,000
Equals Profit: $50,000

If you are not using your own cash, then this typical example of estimating your profit is completely wrong! The deal sounded quite good, and the guy will even finance the deal for you, but you need to take off the rose-colored glasses for a moment.

Always ask how much the *financing* will cost you. I want to use an example that I was taught once in a financial class that my wife and I took a few years back. We were told to always ask what the financing will cost, and we were trained to understand the true cost of borrowing money.

Now I want you to visualize in your mind the last time you purchased a couch for a moment. Did you see the advertisement in huge letters on the front of the store that said, "No Money Down, Same As Cash?" These ads are a scam and I will tell you why.

The furniture retailer structures the purchase and financing of the couch to get you in the door. They have figured out that the average consumer has not saved up ahead of time to buy a couch that will cost $3-5K on average. So, they tease you with this ad that allows you to get the couch now and pay it off in 36 months, with 0% interest during the 3-year time period. They also happen to know something you don't. They know that 95% of consumers do not pay off the loan in the 36 months they have given you. So, they set the default rate close to 30% after the initial same-as-cash time period. Furniture companies found out a long time ago that they can earn more money from lending than from selling couches.

Gamblers rarely beat the house and consumers rarely beat the lender. As it says in Proverbs, "the borrower is slave to the lender." Your typical hard-money lender, which is what sellers like this really are, will charge you the going real estate industry rate of 15% simple interest plus 3 points for originating the loan. The 3 points count as 1 interest point each, so the loan is really 18% interest. The loan is also not amortized and is an interest-only loan. They are not including principal payments here, so you are not paying the loan off as you go. When you consider the average fix-and-flip deal takes six months to complete, the hard money can get very expensive very quickly.

Now let's revisit our example deal and see how the hard money fits in:

After-Repair Value (ARV): $285,000
Less Purchase Price: -200,000
Less Repairs: -35,000
Equals Estimated Profit: $50,000
Less Points Paid Upfront: -6,750
Less 6-Month's Interest: -16,875
Projected Net Income: $26,375
This deal doesn't sound so great anymore, does it? We haven't even

paid the real estate agents yet or any of our closing costs, and we are already close to half of the profit we originally thought we'd earn. Once you consider 6% ($17,100) to pay both of the real estate agents, and a conservative 2% ($5,700) to pay your closing costs, you are left with almost no profit in this deal. You'd net about $3,500—even though you spent the last six months working on it!

Did you know that your typical VA and HUD buyers will usually ask you to pay their closing costs? This is actually very common and their lenders will even use it as a sales tactic to get the buyer to do business with them. These buyers who failed to save up for their own down payment and closing costs will ask you for another 2-4% of the sales price. Sounds a lot like the "No Money Down, Same as Cash" example, doesn't it?

Many novice investors will quickly succumb to the emotional aspects of doing these types of deals. Hey, to be honest, it can happen to anyone. When you visit the property, you are greeted by a half dozen other investors who are all scrambling to get their offers in. Everyone's acting like this is the deal of the century, and you know you will need to bid aggressively to get this one. However, I hope that when your boots hit the ground and your emotions are running high, you'll stop for a moment and consider the lending aspect of these deals. You can still earn profit doing these types of deals, but if you are going to borrow expensive money, plan for the worst and try to buy the property for a cheaper price.

How to Structure Lending Where Everyone Wins

If you want to structure deals where everyone wins, please consider partnering up. You usually need cash to compete in this arena, so why not find a private money lender and split the profits? You'll do a whole lot better in the long run, and you can greatly reduce your risks by doing so. When you consider partnering with another person, you need to always think long and hard about what each partner brings to the table. If one partner has the money to lend, then the other partner will need to bring some skill and expertise to the partnership.

A lender may team up with a contractor as these are two of the biggest costs in a typical fix-and-flip deal. A lender may also partner with a real estate agent since this is another large cost. Whether you decide to be the lender yourself or partner with one, you need to always think about the profit in each deal and make sure there is enough to go around.

If you lend money on deals, as we have said previously, make sure this is a property you would be okay with personally owning. I have seen lenders like Mr. Daniels lend money on a fix-and-flip deal and then end up owning it themselves. He was perfectly fine with taking the property back because he knew he could still rent it out each month and earn a positive return on his money.

Whether you are the borrower or the lender, I want you to really take the topic of this section to heart. Always, and I mean *always*, structure deals where everyone wins. Your most valuable asset in the real estate business is your reputation. If you are doing aggressive deals and ripping people off, eventually no one will want to do business with you. We are all in this business to earn a healthy profit, so don't be aggressive, and make sure you build solid win-win relationships. If you can nail this mentality, you will be able to easily quit your day job and feed your family for years to come.

CHAPTER 5

Building a Turn-Key REI Business

Adam and I have built a successful turn-key real estate investment (REI) business over the years, and we've also managed to build up an impressive portfolio of properties. We have combined my skill as a wholesale buyer and renovation contractor with Adam's business and marketing expertise to form our real estate investment company, Locklear Real Estate Partners.

We purchase residential homes at below wholesale value, renovate them, place them with professional management, and then sell them to investors. Our buyers are, for the most part, busy professionals or retirees who have cash to invest. Our customers enjoy 9-13% net returns, and about one-third of our properties are sold to overseas dealers. These dealers, who we call our "strategic partners," purchase our homes and then re-market these investments to customers in their home countries.

Building a turn-key real estate investment business can be very profitable and rewarding. Our small business not only supports our families but also the families of our renovators, subcontractors, and other small businesses. Last but not least, we enjoy the positive feeling that comes from taking the ugliest home in a neighborhood and transforming it into one of the nicest. The end result is a great home for a middle-class family, a good living for us and our associates, a good profit for our strategic partners, and fantastic, safe returns and tax write-offs for the final investors or rental property owners. If structured correctly, this can truly be a win-win-win-win business.

As with every other real estate path, there are negatives to becoming a turn-key provider. It takes a solid commitment and perseverance to build any successful business. Not only do you need to understand real estate, but you must also become an expert buyer, rehabber, and marketer. Financing is not as hard to obtain as you might think, however. We have developed a system where all the costs of our acquisitions and renovations are financed by the final buyers.

Becoming a turn-key provider is more of a destination than a starting point. I began as a wholesaler and gradually progressed to a turn-key operation. If you are willing to spend the time and effort to build a multi-faceted business, providing turn-key investments can be very profitable. Just don't underestimate the assets and abilities you will need for success in this field.

From 1982 until 1986, I was a full-time real estate entrepreneur. My partner and I specialized in providing break-even cash flow properties to high-income professionals. During those years, we enjoyed accelerated depreciation, and you could write off 185% depreciation in year one. Our buyers would refinance the properties to a neutral cash flow, then use the depreciation and interest deduction to shelter other earned income. The end result was that an owner could profit around $4,000 per house with little or nothing invested. They could also expect future appreciation. We had built a business that paid each of us a $36,000 annual salary, which believe it or not was pretty good money back in the 1980s.

A few years later, Congress passed the Tax Reform Act of 1986 and killed accelerated depreciation write-offs. Shortly afterward came the Savings and Loan Crisis, and my partner and I were effectively put out of business overnight. We were able to retain around 30 rental properties; however, those properties were all secured by mortgages. My partner and I got together and discussed our options. He wanted to keep the rentals and I wanted to sell them at cost. The main reason I wanted out was that I was the field guy and would have to maintain the houses. We eventually came to terms and agreed to an amicable parting. He got 30 rental properties, and I got the Sea Ray boat and motorhome we had owned together. My partner later dumped the properties and left the real estate business. He now operates a successful retail business and we remain friends to this day. As for myself, I spent the next 15 years in the commercial construction business.

In 2001, I was working a job as a senior project manager and was right in the middle of a 12-million-dollar project. I was very good at my job, but I was bored to death. Right after the September 11th attack, I simply gave my two-weeks notice and walked away. My best friend told me I was nuts, my wife, Suzette, was scared to death, and the kids asked me if they would still get Christmas presents.

In 2002, I sold 52 houses as a wholesaler with an average markup of $5,000. Now, I was not really a newbie to real estate as I had obtained my real estate license in 1979, and between 1982 and 1986, I had immersed myself in real estate education. For the next few years, I prospered as a real estate wholesaler. My wife was able to quit her job working for the State of Florida. I also began to buy a lot of toys, including race cars, boats, motorcycles, recreational vehicles, and more. We moved from our 1,800 SF home into our present 6 bedroom, 4 bath, 4,300 SF home. Wholesaling has been very good to me and my family.

In the early 2000s, the real estate market was stable, but around 2004, things began to really heat up. Just about anyone with a heartbeat could qualify for a mortgage, and values were increasing every year. I began to both buy and build single family housing. Over the next two years, I don't believe I sold one house as a wholesaler, and my income from building and selling new homes was actually even better than what I was making during my wholesaling years. My son Adam was my real estate agent, and I had hired a full-time construction manager. Everything was cruising along, almost on autopilot.

In early 2006, I began to hear rumors that a slowdown, maybe even a "crash," was coming. I shrugged off the warnings. After all, this was Florida where real estate values never decline. It couldn't happen here. Boy was I wrong! We named this one the "Mortgage Crisis." When it hit, there were no buyers who could obtain loans for my houses. I was stuck with about 15 houses with construction loans that I could not sell. I had to dump them at substantial losses. I probably lost $500,000 in cash. It took me several years to recover, but I did recover.

I did not leave the business, but I did adapt to the market changes. I found new buyers with cash. Most were busy professionals with great jobs and high incomes. These buyers had no interest in rehabbing or managing properties. They just wanted to cash-in on the foreclosure bargains and build their retirement accounts.

My son Adam was not only my real estate broker but had founded and was operating a thriving property management company. The founding of our company was a natural progression which soon led us to acquisition, renovation, management, and marketing. Our segregated operations quickly evolved into a turn-key rental property provider business. Adam and my wife, Suzette, are my partners in this business. We retained Community Building & Restoration, Inc. (a general contracting company), Remodel Right, Inc. (a remodeling company), and Locklear Realty as subsidiary companies.

While it may sound big and complicated, it boils down to the three of us in ownership and management, supported by subcontractors. We have no employees and no board of directors. We don't borrow money (not even on credit cards), and we operate these business on a 100% cash basis. It took us some time to figure out the secret to keeping our turn-key real estate business primed and steadily producing income. We eventually developed a sales pipeline and order of operations for success. We use this same formula on every deal we do and it works beautifully.

Here's how it works:

1. We offer real estate investing education and personal mentoring to consumers. These services add potential investors to our private email list.
2. We search out and place homes under contract that meet our preset criteria and are located in our target neighborhoods. We buy these properties in order to provide our customers with a 9-13% NET spendable return (after paying for all expenses, including renovation, closing costs, tenant placement, and professional management).
3. We offer these homes for sale to our private clients via our email list. Our offer includes a walk-through video, a detailed renovation estimate, and a pro-forma statement that analyzes the investment over a 10-year period.
4. Our buyers sign purchase and renovation contracts, and we move smoothly through the closing process, which includes a full title investigation and title policy, closing settlement statement, and property insurance commitment.
5. After everything clears, we close the purchase. Our customer actually buys the property and places the renovation funds in escrow with the title company. We draw the remodeling funds out in arrears as the renovation progresses (usually over 3-5 weeks).
6. Once renovation is completed, the customer is referred to our property management partners and a tenant is re-

cruited, screened, and placed. Each month, the net rent is directly deposited into the owner's bank account.

Our business process has evolved to provide a true hands-off, passive investment for our clients. These clients include doctors, attorneys, professionals, middle-class working couples, retirees, school teachers, and even international investors. We do have competition in this business, and our main competitors probably sell 4-5 times the number of houses that we do each year—and at prices about 20-30% higher than ours. They do, however, fund their company with borrowed money, spend a ton on advertising, and have 20-30 full-time employees. The type of properties we provide are nearly identical to theirs, but our low overhead keeps our prices down and our clients' returns up.

I don't have anything bad to say about our competitors. Many of them were once my students. Some of them have built reputable and successful companies. They do things their way and we do things our way. Neither operation is good or bad—just different.

We usually have more buyers waiting in line than properties to sell. Our average time from broadcasting an available property to signing a contract with a client is less than 24 hours. Our only advertising is our monthly Meetup group and a few website links. This is what the turn-key business is all about. While very lucrative, it requires that you commit to building a business that fits your abilities. You will need to do what you do best and pay others to do the rest. It can be a small business, medium sized, or a fully funded large business. That is your decision to make. Most turn-key businesses are the result of a natural progression from wholesaling and renovating to providing turn-key rentals.

Consider Building a Turn-Key Real Estate Business

To be successful, you will need a very well-rounded bank of experience and the ability to locate, renovate, and market turn-key investment properties. Adam and I earn a very healthy living in this business. It's not uncommon to earn multiple six-figure incomes running a turn-key real estate company. My background is heavily technical in the construction, project management, and engineering fields. Having also spent several years in housing investment sales, my education has been vital to my success in the turn-key business.

Adam earned degrees in business and economics and is a licensed real estate broker, property manager, and business broker. His real expertise is in finance, real estate acquisition, business development, and marketing. I am not implying that you need to be just like us. You will, however, need to understand acquisition, renovation, finance, property management, business development, and marketing to succeed in this field. Most successful turn-key providers have spent many years building their expertise, and I know of none who actually *began* in the turn-key business. Most of us started as real estate wholesalers and later progressed into providing turn-key rental properties. You might want to consider finding a partner who can complement your abilities.

Adam's Take on Turn-Key Real Estate

I love what we do so much. I tell my wife every week that I have the greatest job on the planet. It was just recently that I wrapped up a long weekend with the family in the Appalachian Mountains. We had spent a few days hiking waterfalls and climbing rocks with our ever-energetic toddlers. My wife asked me on a Sunday if we needed to return home so I could get back to work. I told her, "Hang on honey, I just need to check my bank accounts and spreadsheets real fast on my phone." I whipped out my iPhone right there—a mile up into the mountains—while sitting on a giant rock face, and covered in dirt from the cave exploring we had just done. I opened my business bank account via one app and quickly double-checked my company books on another. Then I opened Gmail and accessed my Google Docs to check the closing production of our upcoming deals that week. Finally, I closed my phone, smiled at my wife, and said, "We can stay a few more days, sweetheart. I just closed a deal last night and the money has funded. We have two more deals closing tomorrow, and the funds will post by Thursday." She calmly smiled back and we scooped up the kiddos and proceeded to hike back down the mountain.

Wow, what an amazing business, right? Well, running your own company does give you certain freedoms, but it's also a lot of busy work, and you have to be completely committed. If I wanted to sell you an education package, right about now I would be asking if you wanted to learn how to work from home in your pajamas, earn six figures, and travel the world while your business ran itself. But this scenario is just a little far fetched. The reality is I do get to work in my PJs, and I do leave on weekdays to climb mountains with my family, but I also worked like a madman to get to this level. The week before I left for vacation, I logged over 60 hours meeting with clients, teaching investors how to do profitable deals, networking with high-net-worth individuals, training virtual assistants, writing sales manuals, packaging deals, and performing a myriad of other tasks that require my personal touch to run a successful turn-key real estate business.

Joe and I know what tasks can only be performed by one of us, as the actual business owners, and what tasks we can hire vendors or virtual assistants to perform. We have been able to identify and break down these tasks because we have stripped our entire business apart and attempted to outsource every piece of it at one time or another. We wholeheartedly believe in working smarter instead of harder. Sometimes that means hiring an assistant to do routine tasks. Other times it means getting in your car and touring a property personally to get a feel for the deal.

You never really get to just 100% automate a turn-key real estate business. It's just too technical and there is too much on the line for your client if you screw up. If your employee flips a burger wrong or pours the wrong drink at your fast food chain, you just dump it out and get them another one. The loss is aggravating, but of minimal damage. However, if your assistant screws up a real estate contract or your contractor underestimates the amount of repairs the home needs, it can cost you thousands upon thousands of dollars. This doesn't mean that you can't have partners who are highly skilled and qualified individuals to complete these important tasks. But it does mean that you'd better think long and hard about the scalability of your business when forming partnerships.

The Locklear Partners Turn-Key Real Estate Business Model

My partnership with Joe has worked well because we complement one another. We each have different skill sets that we bring to the table, and we trust one another completely. To simply break down our partnership, Joe is the contractor and I am the real estate broker. Now, we do so much more than that, but on paper that is who we are. We have found that our partnership maximizes profit by having Joe handle the entire renovation side of the business. This includes Joe viewing motivated seller properties and bank foreclosure listings to estimate the amount of repairs needed.

On the other side, I handle all the brokerage-related activities. I organize and run all of our online and direct mail marketing required to generate leads to bring in the deals. I am also responsible for submitting all the offers, writing sales contracts with sellers and banks, working real estate closings, and selling the property to our end buyers. Joe has built a renovation crew to fix up the properties and has project managers who run his renovation jobs. I have built a marketing, sales, and real estate team to handle my side. We each are cross-trained on the other partner's job, and there is a degree of overlap we have baked into our business model to hold one another accountable.

We make it a priority to meet face to face once per week so each partner can ask the other about his side of the business. I will often meet with Joe to get an update on how the renovation jobs are coming along and what expansion or contraction is needed with the renovation crews to effectively balance his side. Joe will ask me about our marketing and get an update on how much inventory the banks are holding at the time. He also asks me what response our marketing is getting per mailing and how effective we've been that week working with the banks. If one partner believes there is something the other partner can do to improve his side, he will say so at the meeting. It can be tough sometimes hearing the hard, cold truth when you are busting your butt to improve your side, but, in the end, I wouldn't have it any other way. The accountability aspect of having a great business partner ultimately makes us better at what we do.

Why Having Two Partners and Not Three Has Worked for Us

There are, of course, only two formal business partners within our company. Our wives are honestly the true heroes behind closed doors, but for all intents and purposes, there are only two partners at Locklear Real Estate Partners. If you plan on having three or even four or more partners, you will have a very hard time getting to a six-figure income with a turn-key real estate investment business. In my experience, by the time you use up your 40-hour work week and get deals done that month, you just won't have enough profit to split with more than one partner.

The decision-making process will also become quite complicated if you add that third partner. In my humble opinion, the only time you should add a third partner for a turn-key real estate business is if you want to bring in a money partner and expand. If you plan on bringing in a lender, please understand they will be a partner. The reason they will become a partner, even if you borrow commercial funds, is due to the fact that you will be forced to grow. If you decide to borrow private funds, that lender will have a direct say in what you do.

Now I know you can bring in a silent partner who just puts up the money and let's you make all the day-to-day business decisions, but run your business into the ground and see how silent they remain. Please do understand that our philosophy was never to build a medium- to large-sized company. We knew from day one that we wanted to stay small. We figured out that there wasn't enough profit in our local market if we grew quickly and that we would have to expand into other markets to justify growing over 10-15 employees. This fact is due to inventory. There are only so many houses that you can earn a profit from fixing up and renting out within a specified geographic location.

If you grow rapidly and corner your local market, you will eventually have to move to a new market, or you will be forced to build new homes. When we considered how long it would take to grow, we figured by the time we expanded to building new homes, the market would get soft again and bounce us back to where we started. So, why kill ourselves? Instead of doing all that work, we can simply run a lean and profitable small business and crank out enough profit each year for two partners. Staying small also allows us to adapt quickly and remain a debt-free business.

How Mastering Supply and Demand Maximizes Profit

The key to getting good and hitting the sweet spot on profit in the turn-key real estate business is mastering supply and demand. It's very much like a seesaw. On one side are your buyers. They want to earn cash flow on rental properties. They want to take their funds out of their IRAs, bank accounts, and under-performing stocks and put them into real estate. The problem is they are scared to do so. It's your job to educate them on why they should trust you to purchase one of your properties. Once you master this, you will have too many buyers on that side of the bench. They will constantly weigh you down and demand good deals that you just don't have. At this point, you are putting too much energy into these buyers. Your problem is a good one now. You have more demand than supply. Now it's time to go get some houses.

This brings us to the other side of the seesaw—your houses. You have learned what a good deal is. You know how much repair is needed to make the place rentable. You have learned how to estimate repairs, and you've hired or partnered with a contractor to get the home rent ready. You have even done a few renovations yourself to learn the process, and you're comfortable with a higher level of repairs now. Your marketing system to find good deals is primed, and you have potential new deals coming in daily. It doesn't take long for you to get good deals under contract and then package them to sell.

So, now all you have to do is reach out to your buyers who are waiting for the deals. They should be frothing at the mouth by now, just waiting for that profitable investment you promised them. By loading up on buyers *first* and then going out and getting the deals, you will create a perfect supply and demand formula. You will be able to close more deals and you will be able to close them faster. Once you get this system primed, your bank account is going to explode.

"But, wait a minute," you say, "how do I find the buyers?" If you aren't sure where to find them, I recommend visiting your local real estate investor association (REIA). Just start bringing your deals to meetings and eventually you will find a cash buyer who is looking for a good deal. If you want to learn more intricate systems for finding buyers, just contact Joe and me. We would be happy to mentor you through the process.

What Tasks to Complete Yourself vs. What Tasks to Hire Help For

We have talked multiple times now about balancing partner tasks and employee or vendor tasks. Many business owners will tell you this is one of the most important keys to success when maximizing business profit.

Below are some tasks that we have decided are too important to give to someone else. These important tasks have a direct effect on profit:

- Signing off on final contractor repair estimates
- Developing relationships with foreclosure bank representatives
- Finalizing deals with private sellers
- Developing and adapting our marketing pipeline to buy houses
- Developing and adapting our sales pipeline to sell houses
- Sales calls with potential buyers
- Educating buyers
- Private tours with potential buyers
- Personally holding contractor and real estate broker licenses
- Business systems development and growth strategies
- Research and development
- Managing each partner's business operations

• Managing client interactions with buyers after the sale

Below are some tasks that we have found to be too routine and mundane to require a partner to perform:

1. Pulling MLS listings (initially)
2. Setting up showings with sellers
3. Stuffing letters
4. Placing bandit signs
5. Calling For Sale By Owner properties
6. Basic bookkeeping
7. Billing clients and paying subcontractors
8. Answering initial contact from motivated seller prospects
9. Writing sales letters to buy houses
10. Initially viewing properties to weed out the bad ones
11. Managing day-to-day renovation jobs
12. Inbound marketing, including SEO, pay-per-click ads, and social media marketing
13. Website development and management
14. Sales video production and marketing
15. Outbound marketing, including sales calls and email ads
16. Anything else that costs less than $30 per hour

By successfully identifying tasks and organizing them in a way to maximize profits, you will set your turn-key real estate business up to be successful for many years. In a soft market, you may have to roll up your sleeves and take on more tasks yourself. In a hot market, you will do best to outsource the easy stuff and spend your time with clients who are your actual cash producers, since they have the money to buy your deals. Your task breakdown may look a little different than ours, but make sure you handle tasks that only you can do.

Don't Forget to Invest in What You Sell (the Exit Strategy)

In the end, Joe and I will tell you our end goal is to build a profitable and lasting turn-key real estate business, live below our means, and then invest our disposable income into the same rental properties we sell to our clients. Our pattern for years has been to buy four properties monthly. We typically sell three properties and keep one for the family portfolio. We buy what we sell, and we truly realize the key to long-term wealth building is owning rental property.

Our family got together a few years back and mapped out its exit strategy. Our strategy includes family members owning rental property and then receiving rental income over the course of their lives. We depreciate our rental properties using the normal straight line method of 27.5. The depreciation provides a nice, yearly tax write-off for each property. The only thing to be careful of is that depreciation is recaptured by the IRS upon the sale of the investment property. So, our family decided instead of selling depreciated properties, why not just set them up in land trusts so we can skip probate, keep them repaired and occupied, and have a professional property manager take care of them each month. Each family member will receive $500-$700 cash per property every month in addition to the depreciation deduction. You see, we practice what we preach. We have said it before and I will say it again: Owning free and clear, low-cost, cash flow rental properties is a fantastic and proven way to build wealth in America!

CHAPTER 6

Building a Rental Portfolio

If you want to build real wealth—the kind of wealth that will literally change not only your life but the lives of your family and heirs—then building a rental portfolio is the path I recommend. If you lack the assets and abilities (or think you lack them), you may want to start with another method. But unless you eventually wind up here, you probably won't win the "Monopoly" game.

With every other path we considered, the end result was a "job." While you may own the job, the fact remains—when you quit working, the income disappears. Portfolio building is different from any job. When properly built, a rental portfolio will provide a lifetime stream of hands-off passive income that can easily be passed on to your heirs.

Before getting into the "nitty-gritty" of portfolio building, I want to take a moment to tell you why early in my career I chose to invest in residential single family houses. The term "real estate" has a very wide definition that includes houses, apartments, land, strip malls, warehouses, and more. Broken down even further, houses can range from shotgun shacks in war zones to multi-million-dollar oceanfront mansions. When I hear that "real estate is up" or "real estate is down," it doesn't mean a lot to me. I never invest to take advantage of market changes—I invest for *cash flow only*. I avoided commercial property as I know very little about it. After careful consideration, I decided that there was nothing that could be done with multi-family buildings that I could not do better and safer with single family houses.

More specifically, I like to invest in what I call "bread and butter" neighborhoods. I would describe these as areas where working families will be comfortable living. In my home market, this eliminates high-crime ghettos at the lower end and houses above $80,000 on the higher end. I feel the sweet spot is where rents go for between $700 and $1,000 monthly, and where after-repair values range from about $50,000 up to $80,000 (based on 2017 values in Jacksonville, Florida).

Why I Love the Bread and Butter Market Segment

I like to invest in lower middle-income neighborhoods for a number of reasons. Not only is this demographic the widest segment of the population, but investing in these areas offers a number of advantages. Let's take a look at a few of them.

- **A solid foundation.** In a declining economy, renters will tend to move into lower-cost housing. I don't want to be at the bottom of the pyramid, but I do want to be near the base in what I call "bread and butter" neighborhoods.
- **Diversification.** Unlike multi-family housing, my single family homes are not centralized and therefore are less vulnerable to localized negative events.
- **Easier to resell closer to retail values.** When I decide to sell, I am not restricted to selling to an investor. I can also choose to sell to an owner-occupant at a retail price.
- **Less expensive to acquire.** I have purchased a single family fixer-upper for as little as $6,000. Due to increased competition amongst buyers, multi-family units cost much more, moving the investment cost well above what many new in-

vestors can afford.

- **Dealing with a higher class of tenant.** Compared to multi-family housing, tenants who rent houses are more stable and easier to deal with than renters who will accept apartment living.

I do understand that a lot of the gurus out there encourage their students to "move to the next level" and learn to invest in apartments and commercial properties. I disagree that commercial investing is the natural progression from investing in single family houses. Multi-family and commercial properties have very little in common with houses, and investing in them requires much more expertise, leverage, and risk. I would argue that there is nothing to be gained by moving from houses to apartments and commercial investments. Most gurus who nudge you in this direction are simply looking to sell you more expensive education and training.

The only negative to building a residential single family real estate portfolio that I can think of is the fact that it takes *time*. This is not a "get-rich-quick" scheme. Instead, it's about building a solid, sustainable path to real wealth and financial freedom. As I buy and sell turn-key investments, I always find a few to keep for myself. If you have cash available, there is no better investment than single family managed rentals. Don't overlook converting your IRA to self-directed and investing in homes. Even if you are cash poor, with at least 10 years to retirement, I can show you how to fund a portfolio without banks or partners.

Building a Rental Portfolio for Retirement

I define retirement as "the point where your passive income exceeds your earned income." This is, to me, the optimal retirement point. Now, I know things happen in life and there are many other factors that effect when you will retire. I want to talk mainly about financial preparation for retirement. You may want to retire at age 40 or age 70. When you are able to retire will almost certainly depend on what you have done to build passive income.

Earned income is created by working a job. Self-employment is when you own your job. I define every endeavor that provides earned income as a job. When you can no longer work, your job quits paying you. Now I know you are thinking that jobs provide retirement income, but that is not entirely true. Employers, as a benefit to retain employees, may contribute to your retirement account. Most employers are required to contribute to social security and match your contributions. If you follow traditional retirement investments, your return might grow at a rate of 3-6%. After working 30 or more years, you *might* retire with a passive retirement income at 50-70% of your previous earned income.

For most of us, that's not enough to live on. Portfolio building can be an excellent supplement or replacement for a traditional retirement account. A typical rental portfolio should average between 9% and 13% net returns, allowing you to retire much sooner and with much more spendable income than typical stock-based plans. Many of our clients move their existing IRA funds to invest in income-producing rental real estate.

The process involves converting their IRA to a self-directed account and then investing in houses. The investment must be truly passive and conform to all the IRS rules and regulations. It is a very simple process and there is a ton of education and information available on the conversion process. In my opinion, investing with a self-directed IRA is best as you can take advantage of depreciation write-offs and it's more profitable than the stock market where most traditional accounts are invested.

Let's talk a bit about wealth building. Ownership of real estate is the cornerstone of wealth in America. While people build wealth in different ways, the majority of the money almost always winds up invested into real estate. You don't have to inherit money to build wealth this way, either. I personally believe that real estate ownership is absolutely the greatest wealth-building tool available to the average citizen.

In Chapter 8, we will be talking about the basics of real estate ownership to help you understand your rights and responsibilities. But for now, let's focus on the benefits of owning rental properties.

1. **Income.** Rental property will provide you with a regular monthly income.

2. **Appreciation.** Along with monthly income, your property should increase in value over the years. Appreciation is not guaranteed, however, and I would advise you to completely ignore appreciation when analyzing a potential investment. If you get appreciation (historically in Jacksonville, appreciation has averaged 6% annually), then it will be a bonus.

3. **Tax Advantages.** The IRS allows you to take a deduction each year for depreciation, plus if your investment is financed, you can write off part or all of the interest paid. If you own the property for at least a year as an investment, you are allowed a reduced tax rate on the profit earned (capital gains tax treatment).

4. **Leverage.** Leverage can be simply defined as *using other people's money to earn cash or income for yourself.* Getting a mortgage on a property is an example of "leveraging." If you borrow $75,000 to acquire a $100,000 property, you are said to have a loan-to-value (LTV) of 75%. Used judiciously, leverage can be very advantageous. The ultimate

leverage occurs with rental property, as you can borrow money and your tenant pays it back for you. You want to approach leverage cautiously, however, as it can be a two-edged sword. You want to avoid over-leveraging by making sure that your real net spendable income surpasses total expenses by a good, safe margin.

To clarify this further, let me see if I can give you an analogy of real estate income vs. stock investments.

Try walking into your bank and asking for a loan to buy stock. Your banker will smile and ask what other collateral you are willing to put up. Next ask for a loan secured by real estate, and you will find they will gladly make the loan based on the real estate's value. The actual benefits of real estate ownership are so good that, to some, they are almost unbelievable. Go back to the same bank and ask the officer for a loan. Tell them that you would prefer they made the loan to you, but that someone else would pay back the money. Let them know that you want tax write-offs, and when the other person pays off the loan, you want the free and clear collateral deeded to you, not them. Let them know you want to make a small monthly profit, and it would be nice if the collateral also grew in value during the term of the loan. I'll bet you they call over their security guard. Still, what have you just described? It's nothing more than a simple, leveraged, real estate investment.

By now, I am sure you know that building a rental portfolio is my preferred pathway to real estate success. Adam and I make a living providing turn-key properties to other investors. This is our "job," but every penny that we can afford to save is invested directly back into our personal rental portfolios.

Now there are many sub-paths that you can follow to success in the portfolio-building business. Adam and I have differing opinions about the properties we like to own. Our main differences are based on the fact that I am looking to retire within about seven years, and Adam has a good 30-35 years before reaching retirement age. Generally, Adam likes properties at the higher end of our niche. While cash flow is lower on these more expensive properties, he doesn't need the income yet, so he can afford to wait many years for rents and values to increase.

I did not begin holding properties until I was 55 years old, and my retirement income goals are pretty ambitious, so I cannot afford to make mistakes. I absolutely love to create income on free and clear properties, and I will buy the most affordable houses available in the "borderline" neighborhoods. I don't buy in the "war zones" or ghettos, but I seldom buy in the most stable family neighborhoods. I buy for maximum cash flow with no consideration of appreciation.

I am going to explain how and why I like these properties, but before I do, I want to give you some advice...

Do not boast or even talk about the number of properties you own. I have very close friends in the real estate business. I know they own rental properties, but I have no idea how many. The main reason is asset protection. Asset protection is an important subject that we will touch on in Chapter 14, but for now, I want you to know that I will not disclose the number of houses that I own or even where my properties are located. I have spent a lot of effort keeping this information private, and I would suggest that you do the same. Any address or name that I quote will not be the real address or name. The numbers, however, will be true and every deal described will be real.

My wife and I prefer to purchase and remodel homes using cash only. We bought one in my wife's IRA last year for as little as $6,000. We spent $10,000 on renovation, and it rents for $695 monthly. Our net spendable return after management on this property exceeds 33%, and it is free and clear. We buy what we can for cash, but we also borrow money to buy houses. Like I said earlier, we don't deal with banks or brokers and prefer to work directly with individual lenders. We pay a good rate and have no shortage of investors standing by to make these loans.

We placed a home under contract in December of 2013. December is our slowest month and it did not sell by time to close. I decided to keep it and to finance it with what I call our "984" loan program. The 984 stands for 9% interest, amortized over 84 months. This means our lender will earn 9% annual interest, and the entire principle will be repaid within 84 months. We were in that property after renovation for a total of $28,000. We left $5,000 cash in the deal and borrowed $23,000. Our loan payment is $370.05 monthly and our tenant pays $800 monthly. After all expenses, management, and loan payments, we net $149.95 monthly. That represents an initial return on our $5,000 investment of 35.9%. The 35.9% does not mean a lot to me right now, but what really gets me excited is the fact that in another 60 months, this property will be free and clear. At that point, our spendable cash flow will increase by $370.05 to $520 monthly.

On a one-time investment of only $5,000, we will receive $520 monthly for the rest of our lives. When we are gone, our children will continue to receive a monthly payment from our family trust. Just eight of these deals and your passive income will build to $4,000 monthly. How hard and how long do some people work to build a $4,000 monthly retirement income?

In my (sometimes not so humble) opinion, building real estate wealth is less about leveraging money and more about leveraging expertise. Not everybody possesses the experience and temperament needed to operate as I do, but for those of you who do, the low-cost market can become a literal gold mine.

Here are a few of my personal do's and don'ts

DO...

1. Buy for cash flow. If the cash flow is inadequate, do NOT buy the property.
2. If you can't collect the rent, $1 is too much to pay. Never buy houses in ghettos.
3. Hire professional property management. Spend your time building wealth, not repairing toilets.
4. Hold properties long term.
5. Buy only structurally sound houses and repair them to top standards.
6. Guarantee long-term tenancy by keeping rents reasonable and providing prompt property maintenance.
7. Approach the property-buying decision armed with the real picture of probable expenses.

DON'T...

1. Become a "landlord." Landlords become unhappy people and many leave the business. Those who like landlording and stay in the business are just weird. (Remember Mr. Roper?)
2. Borrow more than the property can pay back. Leave a monthly margin of at least $150, and keep the length of payments to a minimum.
3. Confuse owning a bunch of properties with building a sound passive income. Your portfolio is only worth the income that it produces. I would choose to own a few free and clear properties over owning a lot of financed property.

To sum up rental portfolio building, I personally believe that the ultimate investment is bread and butter housing, located in middle-class working neighborhoods, owned free and clear or with short-term financing, low LTV, privately financed, and profession-ally managed. My entire retirement is invested in this very specific market. Buying and selling real estate is no different than any other job. If, however, you can learn how to utilize real property to create passive income, you can create a bright financial future for yourself and a generous estate to pass on to your heirs. The real key to success is not leveraging *money*, it's leveraging *expertise*.

Consider Building a Real Estate Rental Portfolio

If your goal is to become filthy rich, this is the path you will need to follow. If retirement income is your main goal, this is also your best choice. The amount of time you have until retirement will be a major factor in how you approach this business. If you have 20 years until retirement, success here is virtually assured if you even moderately apply yourself. However, if you are 60 years old and short of cash, it will be difficult to build a profitable rental portfolio in such a short time.

If you have already built wealth in another field, converting your money to real estate equities can easily provide you with 9-13% net spendable returns, plus tax savings and capital gains tax treatment when and if you sell. 1031 tax deferred exchanges offer further ben-efits once your portfolio is well established.

There are two main sub-paths here: You can become a landlord or a true passive investor. I much prefer and endorse the passive inves-tor route, but we will discuss that in more detail later in the book.

Adam's Take on Rental Portfolios

My wife's and my own retirement income will come in the form of owning nice, affordable rental properties in Florida. I have watched my family and many of our clients purchase small, ugly houses over the years. They will usually look like a bomb went off inside as they are always trashed, located in a marginal neighborhood, and probably make you want to throw on a gas mask to protect yourself from the rancid smell.

It took me some years to wrap my mind around the fact that these were the "bread and butter" houses my dad kept telling me about when I was a kid. I can remember the first time I took a trip to view these bread and butter houses. Joe drove this big black pickup truck and it was really loud. It had one of those giant diesel engines and you could hear him coming a mile away. I can still envision us getting off the highway and pulling on to MLK drive. The environment changed quickly. I saw some guys rolling dice against a wall behind a liquor store and people seemed to just walk right into the street. I asked my dad if he had accidentally hit anyone, and he just smiled and said, "No son, they usually just get out of the way." I must admit I was a little scared. I had just watched an Ice Cube movie with my cousin, and there were plenty of gangsters on the streets in that movie. I swore I was staring at some of them as we drove deeper into the ghetto. Then, just like someone flipped on a light switch, it all changed. We turned down a new street and I saw brand new houses being built. I saw a beautiful park and a new school with plenty of amenities on campus. A small group of children were all playing a game of kickball at the end of a cul-de-sac and the entire area felt different. My dad, Joe, explained to me that sometimes you have to drive through the ghetto to get to a great investment area. Many investors make the mistake of stereotyping a zip code due to crime. The problem with that is you are assuming that the entire zip code has the same problems and that you cannot buy, fix up, and own a great investment property in the area. The truth is, most of the hidden gems in your city lie on the other side of a dirty ditch, and the only way you are ever going to get to them is to drive through the ghetto.

In the future, I began to see these neighborhoods and their surrounding areas through a new lens. It wasn't until I started to understand the numbers—and how investments on this side of town can earn you money every month—that I began to understand why Joe called this area his "bread and butter" real estate investments.

Why Buying Affordable Cash Flow Rentals Is Better Than Guessing on Your Future

Anticipated appreciation is a term that never gets used in real estate investing. So, what exactly does it mean? Well, anticipated appreciation is when you guess about what future real estate prices and values will be. Hedge funds love this strategy, but they'll never use the term directly—mostly because it would scare the pants off any potential clients wanting to invest in the fund. In short, you are gambling on your future by anticipating that values that are currently rising will continue to rise as time goes on. Let's run through an example to cement this scenario.

123 Main Street
3 bedroom/2 bath brick home, 1,500 SF
(Class B neighborhood, low unemployment rate, high-job-growth city with median age of 35)
Expected Net Return: 12%
Current Value: $200,000
Monthly Rent: $1,500
Previous 12-Month Value Growth: 12%
5-Year Expected Growth: 12%
5-Year Expected Value: $352,468.33

In this scenario, we are in a healthy real estate market. The unemployment rate is low, job growth is good in our city, and the future looks great. We have experienced 12% value growth during the previous 12 months, and the real estate market shows no signs of slowing down. It seems like every day another neighbor places their home for sale and cashes out on the home they purchased a few years back. People are refinancing their homes and buying expensive cars and boats and just having a blast as the market roars.

They take some of their disposable income and they invest in real estate. Then they meet with a hedge fund manager who goes over so many graphs and charts that it makes their heads spin. He eventually just pulls out a pencil and paper and goes through this simple, real-life example of what their money will do in five years if they invest in his fund. Now, step on the brakes, put down the checkbook, and *do not* set up the banking auto-draft yet. There is just one big problem here, Mr. Hedge Fund. You forgot about the 800-pound gorilla in the room, dude! What if values do *not* go up 12%?

We'll come back to that scenario in a moment, but Mr. Hedge Fund made another mistake. He didn't properly analyze the deal for us. He was too eager to sell us on future appreciation that he forgot to analyze the cash flow potential of the deal. He should have calculated the cash on cash net return for this investment. So, let's take a moment and run through that analysis.

123 Main Street
3 bedroom/2 bath brick home, 1,500 SF
Purchase Price: $200,000
Monthly Rent: $1,500
Property Management Expense: $150 (10% of monthly rent)
Vacancy and Collection Losses: $75 (5% of monthly rent)
Reserves and Maintenance: $75 (5% of monthly rent)
Property Insurance: $75 (2017 numbers in good rental city)
Property Taxes: $232 (2% of assessed value)

*Now, let's run these numbers again. This time, taking everything
into account.*
$1,500 Total Rental Income
– $607 Total Monthly Rental Expenses
= $893 Monthly Net Income
893 x 12 months = $10,716 Yearly Net Income
10,716 / 200,000 = 5.4% Yearly Net Return

So, our cash on cash net return was only 5.4% net, which is *less
than half* of what we expected. Why does this matter? Well, let's go
back and think about our 800-pound gorilla for a moment.

If values continue to rise at 12% for the next 5 years, then we
can just forget about the gorilla and go out and spend the money
we make during year one. We can travel abroad, buy a luxury car,
and kick the can down the road. Life will be good and we still have
four more years of growth. But, the truth is, markets hardly ever do
exactly what we think they will do. What if the market doesn't go
up? Now you are gambling on your family's future, and here's why.

Inflation happens as markets rise. If inflation is healthy, it will be
between 3-5%. So, your 5% investment barely beats inflation, and
that's only if the market continues to rise. If we have a recession,
values will go down. Businesses will be forced to close their doors
and the unemployment rate rises. When this happened in 2008,
many tenants who were renting homes in the $200,000 range lost
their jobs. As vacancies rose in the $200K neighborhoods, rents went
down. This is simple supply and demand. Your $1,500 per month
unit now only rents for $1,200-1,300 per month. By now, you are
earning only 3%, but something else happens. The invisible hand of
the marketplace corrects itself and real estate values stabilize.

Back in 2008, residential real estate prices took a huge nosedive as
homeowners lost their houses. Bank foreclosures became abundant

and prices went down. By the time a recession happens, you will have no cash flow, and, to make matters worse, you'll actually have *negative* equity growth on your $200K investment home. Markets fluctuate from time to time, so you need to have a double digit net return on rental property investments to make them profitable in the long run.

Now, do you understand why Joe and I love low-cost homes in the mid-low income neighborhoods? When a recession happens, a large influx of tenants will move down into housing where rents go for less than $1,000 per month. Our rental prices actually rise in good markets and bad. Our properties still do appreciate at a normal 5-6% over the long term, and we are getting 12-15% net returns in any market. Buying true bread and butter rental homes in cheap markets is the proven recipe for building long-term wealth in real estate.

How to Find Bread and Butter Investments in Affordable Neighborhoods

If you want to find the best investments, then you really need to know where to look. How do you ensure when you lift up a rock that a diamond will be there instead of a snake? Well, luckily enough for you, Joe and I have turned over plenty of rocks with snakes under them. We have learned through the School of Hard Knocks how to identify these diamonds without even having to flip the rocks over. We have spent our careers learning what areas we like to invest in and what areas to avoid.

I recommend starting your search by talking to your local real estate agents and property management companies. Ask them which areas of town they do not like selling in or renting out units. In Jacksonville, Florida, without hesitation, they will tell you it's the north side of town. If you dig deeper, they will give you specific zip codes that they will call the ghetto, or war zones, or something else that sounds horrible. Believe it or not, these are the areas that you want to hone in on to find the best deals.

Once you get them in mind, your next step is to find a reputable property management company (PM) that manages within these zip codes. They need to have enough units that they are making a splash in the area. If they have less than 30-50 units, do not waste your time. Do not assume that there are no reputable PMs in the area. Professional property managers exist in every single zip code in America.

Next, you are going to call them up and interview them on the phone or step inside their office to pick their brain. Tell them you are looking to buy some investment homes in the zip codes you have chosen and you need to line up a PM ahead of time. They will jump at the opportunity to pick up a new portfolio and client. Next, you will probe them and try to get them to help you learn the area. Your job is to find out which neighborhoods within a zip code a family will live in, and which areas they will not. Remember, this is not your actual family. This is a low-mid income family or a working single parent who wants a clean home in a relatively safe area to live in. It all comes down to this. If you can collect rent and keep the property from getting beat up, then you will have an investment that will produce income.

A good property manager will know which neighborhoods within the zip code will allow for renting to families. Many times you will find out it can be street by street. I like to call them micro-neigh-borhoods here in Jacksonville, due to the fact that their status can change very rapidly. Understanding the geography is your key to success. Bring a map with you and circle the areas within the zip code that will work for you.

I recommend interviewing 3-5 property managers until you find the right fit for your investments. Spend some time driving through the areas in your car so you can start to learn the streets. By the time you finish interviewing your fifth property manager, you will start to learn the neighborhoods. Once you learn the neighborhoods, go out and target cheap, undervalued properties that you can buy at a discount, fix up, and rent out. This hands-on strategy works very well and will help you create tons of value within your personal cash flow rental portfolio.

How to Automate Your Rental Portfolio

In the past, I owned a property management company. When I graduated from college, my dad asked me if I wanted to work for the family company. I was planning on attending graduate school to become either an attorney or an economist. It was a tough choice, but I had always wanted to be an entrepreneur and go to work for myself. I knew working for the family company was the easiest way to get started, and I was eager to begin earning a full-time income.

So, after some discussions with my dad, he told me the position that he had open at the time was property management. It would be my job to show rental units, perform background checks, write leases, collect rent, order repairs, stay in contact with the property owners, and balance the books on a monthly basis. I eagerly agreed to the position. It sounded good, but I had never actually spoken to tenants, and, to be honest, I had no idea what I was getting into.

Later that year, I was managing close to 50 rental units. Word had gotten out that the Locklears now had a full-time property manager and that they could manage your rental units. In reality, my good ole dad had figured out that he could wholesale more investment properties to buyers if we offered property management as part of the package.

It didn't take long for me to hate my job. I had pissed off tenants with repairs they wanted fixed immediately. I had livid property owners who wanted their pesky tenants to stop requesting so many repairs. My tenants constantly accused me of "working for the landlord," and swore that I was never on their side. My landlords were yelling at me and stating, "You are too soft on these tenants. You need to grow a pair."

Needless to say, I became a punching bag. It didn't take long for my stress level to shoot through the roof. Low-income tenants almost cost me my real estate career. If I hadn't gotten some help back then, I probably would have quit this line of work altogether. Later in the book, I'll tell you more about how I grew that property management business, made it a success, and finally sold it for loads of cash, but for now, I just simply want to emphasize one simple principle:

Do not manage your own rental properties!

Let me say that again so it sinks in. *Under no circumstances should you ever consider managing your own rental units.* Do you like grey hair? Do you enjoy acid reflux? When is the last time you strolled down to your local fast food joint and ordered the #1 with a large side of stress? If you manage your own rental property, you will in effect be ordering yourself a large slice of "I don't want to sleep at night" pie. Save yourself endless hours of headaches and hire a professional property manager. Just pay them the going market rate to manage your rentals, and then sit back and enjoy the cash flow for years to come.

Hiring a professional property manager is the only way to truly automate your rental portfolio. It doesn't really matter if you buy cheap, wood-frame homes in bread and butter neighborhoods or fancy, brick masonry homes on the ritzy side of town. Class A tenants will drive you crazy just as fast as Class C tenants. By purchasing real estate at a discount, fixing it up to an appropriate level of repair—and then hiring a professional property manager to screen and place tenants and manage the rental unit—you will be maximizing your returns. Once you have a nice unit with a good family living there, your property manager will handle any problems that arise. You will sleep great at night knowing that you have transferred the stressful part of the business over to a professional who is properly equipped to deal with it.

Now that you have fully automated your first rental house, you will soon be ready to find deal number two. Eventually, you'll have built a 10-unit portfolio, a 50-unit portfolio, and so on. Owning cash flow rentals is the truest way to build lasting wealth. We want you to dream as big as you can here. Let's build enough wealth to make it last for multiple future generations. How fulfilled would you feel if you could leave income to your children, grandchildren, and even your great-grandchildren? Now, that's what we call a dynasty!

Let's close this chapter out by running through a quick exercise. I don't want to get too spiritual on you here, and no, I am not trying to hypnotize you either. Trust me, that is way above my paygrade, but I do want you to envision what life will be like with a fully auto-mated, cash-producing real estate rental business. So, please follow the instructions below, and we will see you in the next chapter!

Please Follow This Exercise to Visualize Your Future Success:

Step 1: Find a quiet place where you can concentrate. If that's not an option, then throw on a good pair of headphones and turn on some soft and slow instrumental-only music.

Step 2: Now get comfortable. You can lean back in your chair, sit at your desk, or even lie down with your hands by your side. If you are driving, please keep your eyes on the road.

Step 3: Now I want you to imagine you are driving down a dusty country road. There isn't a car or person in sight and you begin to relax. As you relax, you see the large oak trees hanging overhead. They have grown so far over the road that their branches are creating a canopy. Now visualize all the fear and stress that is keeping you from investing in real estate. I want you to come up with a visual representation of that fear. If your boss doesn't believe you can do it, then visualize his face. If you are scared of a mean and nasty tenant, then I want you to think about them. If you are worried people will laugh at you for not becoming successful, then please visualize a crowd staring at you.

Step 4: Now, one by one, I want you to hang each of your fears on the branches of that canopy. As you keep driving down the road, hang each problem on a different branch. Please keep driving and keep hanging them one by one onto those branches. As you drive away, you soon forget about them. If you feel the need, you can repeat this step as many times as it takes to get rid of them. Hopefully, after some practice, you will eventually develop a habit of releasing your fears in this way.

Step 5: Now that your fears, problems, and worries are gone, it's time to visualize your future success. Breathe in deeply through your nose, and behind your forehead, visualize a blank space or a white piece of paper. This blank space can be filled with whatever future success you desire. If you desire to earn a six-figure income buying and selling investment property, then visualize this. If you desire to own 100 debt-free, cash-producing rental properties, then picture that. How does it feel getting that rent check deposited into your account each month, when you didn't even have to work hard to get it? What does it feel like to check your bank account and find that it's still loaded with funds, even after all your bills are paid? You're staring at those profitable figures, aren't you, dreaming about that cash in your hand? Dream big and think hard about your future successes. The sky is not the limit and neither are the stars. You can dream as big as you want, and only you can stifle your success. You are fully responsible for any future success you can achieve. The ball is in your court. Now, what are you going to do *today* to get started on that path?

CHAPTER 7

Time to Choose Your Path

As a prerequisite to choosing your real estate investing path, you must understand the difference between *earned income* and *passive income*. Income that is "earned" by working is called "earned income," and this is identifiable by the fact that when you quit doing the work, you also quit receiving the income. Examples of earned income are working a job or working within your own small business. The classification of "passive income" is identified by the fact that the income is not dependent on any current work that you must perform. The income continues coming in as long as the source of the money remains viable. Examples of passive income are income from investments or social security.

When working a job, your "retirement" could be described as the point when earned income ends and passive income begins. You no longer come in to work daily, but you do receive income, usually in the form of a pension, social security, or other retirement account. When working as a real estate investor, however, retirement is often not so easy to define.

Wholesaling, fix-and-flip retailing, and building a turn-key business are great ways to earn income; however, these are active pursuits. Passive income would need to be derived from lending and/or building a rental property portfolio. You will need to build up a large cash reserve before you can become a successful lender, but once you do, you can begin building passive income from day one. As you consider time frames, you need to understand that it takes time to build passive income. Effort that you put forth today to acquire and maintain rental property (especially if using private financing), will produce substantial income 8-10 years in the future.

Unfortunately, many of us don't recognize this fact until we're nearing retirement. If you wait until this critical point, building passive income will become much more difficult. There are things that you can do to compress the time frame, but nothing you can do will replace the income that you could have created by simply beginning earlier. The theme of a good business plan will include a smooth and timely conversion from earned to passive income.

With that in mind, I have a few questions to ask you…

1. How honest are you willing to be with yourself?
2. Can you take a step back and look objectively at your education, assets, and abilities?
3. Do you have a grasp of your real goals?
4. Are your time frames to meet those goals realistic?

If your answers to any of these questions is not an empathetic *yes*, then your chances of success in this or any other endeavor are slim to none. I would encourage you to go back and review the previous chapters. Concentrate on self-analysis and how each path fits in with your current situation. If you feel you have completed a pretty honest evaluation of the above questions, great! Now I want you to write down your answers.

Once you have a solid assessment of your assets, abilities, goals, and time frame, it should be fairly simple to choose your initial path. Remember, you need to choose one methodology to begin with. Looking at the necessary assets, skills, and amount of time involved in each path will help you to choose a technique to meet your current needs. Again, you are choosing a place to *begin*, not your final destination. Once you are successful with your beginning path, your situation will change and other doors will be opened to you. Choosing a single path now will allow you to quickly obtain education specific to the task at hand while greatly accelerating your journey to real estate investing success.

In geometry, a straight line is defined as "the shortest distance between two points." It has been said that the longest distance between two points is called a "shortcut." Never has there been a more accurate statement. Shortcuts lead to disappointment, but an honest assessment of your assets, abilities, and goals—and a realistic time frame—are the building blocks of success.

With that said, go ahead—*choose your path!*

Adam's Take on Choosing a Path

So, you have taken stock of yourself, you know the different real estate investment paths, and now you're beginning to dream about what each path would be like. Or maybe you've been doing this for some time and never really stopped to think about the different paths available to you. With this in mind, let's take a moment to review them again briefly.

1. **You could become a real estate wholesaler.** You would get good deals under contract and then assign the original contract for a fee.
2. **You could become a fix-and-flip retailer.** You would search for undervalued deals that can be bought cheap, fixed up to HGTV standards, and then resold to home buyers who will live there.
3. **You could become a lender.** You would lend your funds out to wholesalers, fix-and-flip retailers, home buyers, or

anyone else you feel is worth lending to. You will want to look at the deals as well in case you end up taking a property back.

4. **You could become a turn-key rental property provider.** You would need to make it a business. This means teaming up with a contractor, a real estate agent, and a lender (if you do not have your own cash).

5. **You could build a rental portfolio that produces double-digit returns.** We recommend that you hire a professional property manager to make your life easier. You could depreciate the investments for 27.5 years and then leave the properties to your heirs, or do a tax-free 1031 exchange and begin the depreciation process all over again.

So, now you have the paths laid out before you. The next step is to do some soul searching and then eventually choose your path. You may try a path or two and find out they're not the one for you. You also may combine paths or decide to do more than one at a time.

I know plenty of lenders who love owning inexpensive, cash flow rental properties. I have a buddy who likes doing one or two fix and flips per year, while his main income comes from wholesaling. You can mix and match or choose as many of these paths as you like. The key to achieving your ultimate future success is getting started *now*.

If you haven't done anything yet, or if your real estate investing game has gotten stale, now is the time to get going. If you aren't happy with what you are currently doing, then you need to try something new. We can't expect to change our current circumstances or improve things by doing the same failed processes over and over. If you want to reach the succulent fruit, you need to learn how to shake the right branches. It's time to choose your path. Now, get out there and shake some branches!

SECTION II

Your Investor Toolbox

CHAPTER 8

Real Estate Basics

Do you really understand the basics of real estate? I believe there are many real estate fix and flippers, landlords, wholesalers, and long-term investors who do not really understand what they're buying, selling, and renting. Most of us, when thinking of real estate we own, might visualize land, grass, buildings, trees, and other physical objects. This may sound crazy to you, but I would contend that we no more *own* the land than a flea *owns* the elephant upon which he sits. The earth existed for billions of years before we were born, and, in all likelihood, it'll exist long after we're gone. We are a vapor, less than the blink of an eye on the face of history. How dare we think we can "own" the earth!

Real estate attorneys understand this fact because, without this knowledge, you cannot understand real estate transactions, documents, or the rights and limitations of what we call "ownership." The actual definition of our modern concept of real property is that it is a "bundle of rights." In America, those rights include:

1. The right to use the property.
2. The right to exclude others from using the property.
3. The right of disposition, which includes the right to sell, grant, or trade the property.
4. The right of inheritance, which means you can decide who gets the property when you die.

While this is a pretty basic explanation, I hope it gets the point across. It may help you to visualize real estate ownership as a bundle of sticks. You can further divide these rights into smaller and more specific bundles, such as mineral and air rights. Various laws and previous agreements can limit your individual property rights. Community association bylaws, the government's right to tax, easements, and eminent domain (the government's right to compensate you and take your land) are all examples of these limitations. To further complicate things, each stick or right can also be transferred for a certain period of time. A lease is a good example of this; the right of possession is transferred for a certain time period.

It is this "bundle of rights" that transfers to the buyer when a property is sold. The legal document that is used to transfer these rights is commonly called a "deed." When is the last time you read a deed from beginning to end? How do you know that the deed actually transferred the rights that you were expecting to get? I know because my title company is an expert at writing and interpreting deeds. They have been closing my deals for over 30 years, and I trust and rely on them 100%. Even if the other party pays for the closing and insists on using their attorney or agent, I still have my own title company do a title search and advise me.

I always want my interest in a purchased property to be "fee simple absolute," which means that I enjoy the entire bundle of rights to the greatest extent possible. I also buy title insurance that insures me against past and future claims upon my ownership rights. Let's look at a few other documents that you need to become familiar with.

Purchase Contract – This is the document that the buyer and seller execute which sets forth all the criteria for the sale. It is this document that instructs the closing agent or attorney on how to process the closing. In Florida, for a contract to be enforceable, it must meet all of the following criteria. An acronym to help you remember is "COLIC."

> **C—Consideration.** This can be money, barter, or some other value given for the property. At least a portion of the compensation must be transferred at the time of contract (binder deposit).
>
> **O—Offer and acceptance.** The seller must agree to sell and the buyer must agree to buy.
>
> **L—Legality of the object.** A contract to sell an illegal object is not enforceable.
>
> **I—In writing and signed.** The contract must be in writing and signed by both parties. This applies only to real estate contracts.
>
> **C—Competent parties.** Both parties must be of legal age and mentally competent.

Other contracts can be expressed or even implied, but real estate contracts must be in writing and signed to be enforceable. I have written real estate contracts on napkins at restaurants. They included all of the above and were completely enforceable.

Lease – A lease transfers the right of possession for a specific time period as declared in the lease document.

Mortgage – This is a document that establishes a security interest in a property. It is used to give the lender the right to take the property if you violate your agreement with them. This document must be recorded with the County Clerk in order to protect the lender's interest. Priority of security interest is set by recording date, with the earlier date having priority.

Note (or Mortgage Note) – This document sets forth repayment terms of the loan. It can be recorded, but recording is not absolutely necessary.

Deed – This document transfers the bundle of rights and should only be prepared by an expert. Three basic types of deeds are commonly used:

1. **General Warranty Deed.** With this deed, the seller guarantees that they own the property in fee simple absolute and that they will defend the buyer's interest against all past or future claims. As a buyer, this is the deed you want. As a seller, never give this deed unless the buyer purchases title insurance. You don't want to be personally responsible for defending the buyer against claims.

2. **Special Warranty Deed.** This deed only guarantees that the grantor has done nothing to create or allow a claim on the property. This deed is commonly used by banks to transfer a foreclosed property.

3. **Quit Claim Deed.** This deed contains no warranty. It simply transfers any interest that the grantor "may" hold. It should not be used for a sale and is commonly used to settle estates and transfer ownership rights between related parties. Unfortunately, quit claim deeds are used by "virtual" wholesalers to flip properties to uneducated buyers when the properties have serious title issues.

I am sure you understand that the above information is just a "primer." Hopefully, however, you now understand that real estate is a "bundle of rights." Before you go into real estate, I want you to have a basic understanding of how those rights are transferred, encumbered, and protected. I also want you to understand that every time the government increases property taxes, or strengthens eminent domain laws, or passes unreasonable environmental protection legislation, you lose a portion of your bundle of rights. We all need to remain alert and do all we can to protect our property rights.

Adam's Take on the Basics

It's very important to understand how real estate works, and yet it's often overlooked by new real estate investors. You need to develop a solid foundation of real estate basics first if you want to achieve long-term success in this industry. Real estate agents know this well because this is one of the first classes you will take when studying to get your real estate sales license.

You don't need to run out and become a real estate agent to succeed as an investor, but you do need to take some time and meditate on the basic crash course Joe just gave you. I have seen so many investors begin buying and selling real estate when they don't even know what they are buying or selling.

When I go to buy a car, I want to pick the brain of the salesman who has the most intimate knowledge of the physical aspects of the car. This salesman needs to be able to talk acceleration and RPMs in detail with me. He needs to know why this year's model is better than last year's—for example, they upgraded the engine—and why the maintenance schedule should be cheaper than this car's direct competitor. I will do research before I get there and basically drool over the car I am interested in online far before I ever set foot on that lot. By the time I do, I can sniff out the scammers and liars who do not actually know their product. I will dismiss them and move on to another salesman. My wife, Patricia, is particularly good at this buying tactic, and the last time we purchased a car for the family, she dismissed six salesmen before finally reaching the floor manager. It was hilarious watching her slice them up like melons and navigating the sales game. She got a great deal that day because she understood the game she was playing, and she had the basic knowledge of what she was buying.

How do you plan to succeed at real estate investing if you do not fully understand the product?

Learn from the Mistakes of a Guy Named Pete

To drill this home, I want to tell you a brief story about a guy named Pete. Pete actually did get his real estate license in Florida, and he quickly hung it with a local real estate broker who owned a national franchise. Pete had been interested in real estate investing for years, and he knew exactly what to do once he got licensed. He ran down to the local real estate investor club and started telling local investors that he had some great leads on tax deed properties. Some of the investors he spoke to had years of experience and politely told Pete they were not interested. Pete insisted that the deals he knew about were really good and could be bought at 50% of value. Every month, he attended the meetings and continued to brag about how much money was being made on these types of deals.

There was just one big problem with Pete's bragging: He'd never actually purchased an investment property, and he really didn't even understand the basic legal aspects of what he was promoting. People love to make money, so eventually a nice couple named Mark and Susie came along and teamed up with Pete. The good news for Pete, who was broke by the way, is that Mark and Susie had plenty of cash. So, they all decided to bid on distressed properties online at the city tax deed auctions. Pete had gotten decent at running sales comps, so they found a good-looking property in a sellable neighborhood and estimated the deal's after-repair value. They had a solid idea of what it would appraise for after they fixed it up. They even found a qualified contractor to renovate the property.

The partners eventually purchased the property from the city, and they were issued the tax deed. There was no previous mortgage on the property to deal with, and they headed out to dinner that night to celebrate the purchase and their vibrant new partnership. When they ran the numbers, they estimated they would net $50,000 in profit, and all they needed to do was complete six projects like this per year, and they could quit their day jobs. It all sounded too good to be true, and that's exactly what it was.

120 days later, they wrote a sales contract on the property with their new home buyers. Pete put together the sales contract and ordered the title search. The next day, Pete got a call from his closing attorney. His attorney had quickly discovered that he and his partners had a bad title. He had been issued a tax deed, but the title was in fact not clear. The new home buyers' lender, a bank, denied lending against any property that did not have a clear title.

Long story short, the buyers were forced to walk, and Pete, Mark, and Susie were stuck with a fully renovated property that they could not sell. They eventually rented the property out to a tenant, but Mark and Susie were very upset with Pete. In their eyes, Pete was supposed to be an expert in real estate. They eventually sued Pete for personal damages and placed a complaint against his license. The last I heard, Pete was fighting them in court and was having personal problems at home.

So, where did Pete go wrong? He'd taken things the extra step by getting his real estate sales license, which is more than many new real estate investors do. But, here's the thing: He thought he had the proper knowledge to go out and do deals, and he quickly became overconfident. He jumped right into a complicated transaction without even understanding it. If Pete would have possessed a basic understanding of deeds and how important clear title is, he would have been fine. He would have identified that the city was not providing a warranty deed and that he would not be able to resell the property to a homebuyer who was obtaining a mortgage from a bank.

You would think that Pete would have been taught all of this in his real estate course. Well, the truth is, they covered deeds quickly, and, unfortunately, he failed to remember deed types when he did this deal. The course also taught him nothing about tax deed sales as it was not part of the curriculum.

How to Use Real Estate Basics to Achieve Long-Term Success

If you want to be successful in real estate investing, you need to study hard on the basics and always think about the bundle of rights when you are doing your deals. If you really want to save some time and learn how to structure the best deals possible, find yourself a really good real estate attorney and run all your deals through them.

Joe and I have a title company that we have used for years. We send all of our potential deals over to them, and we make sure to get a basic title search run before we ever bid on a property at the auctions. When we buy from the banks, we do the same thing, even if they push their own title company on us. We have learned over the years that a bad title can kill your deals. By having a basic understanding of real estate, you can set yourself up for years to come. Hey, the worst-case scenario here is you hire a great real estate attorney—someone you can talk to about your deals who will help you make effective decisions that allow you to earn the highest profit possible.

CHAPTER 9

Determining Values

Before you can determine a property's value, you must first decide on the final use (or disposition) of the property. Common uses for residential properties include rental (portfolio), sale (retail flip), and development. We are going to ignore development as this book is about the first two uses.

Let's begin with a property that would be placed in a rental portfolio. You might be keeping a rental property in your personal portfolio or you might be selling it as a rental property to another investor. The important determining factor is that its final use will be as a rental property.

Valuing Rental Properties

Never base the value of a rental property on any factors other than the net income you'll earn from the property and your desired rate of return. One more time: *Never base the value of a rental property on any factors other than net income and desired rate of return.* You need to get this rule ingrained into your real estate investor psyche.

Now, when I state this rule in any teaching venue, I always get a lot of feedback, such as "what about the type of house?" (i.e. concrete or frame, windows, roof, electric) or "what about the neighborhood? Certainly houses in better neighborhoods are worth more." Remember that I said *net* income. The home's condition and neighborhood are all factors to consider when determining the scheduled gross monthly rental amount. Other factors such as type of construction, exterior finishes, age of the roof, plumbing, air conditioning, and electrical are all considered when setting reserves for replacement and maintenance.

I strongly advise against purchasing a property based on what you *think* it "might" be worth in the future. This is speculation. If you want to speculate, there are a lot of books on playing the stock market, investing in commodities, and real estate development. This book focuses on buying, holding, and selling residential real estate. Now, in this life, there are few guarantees, but investing in single family housing in "bread and butter" neighborhoods, based on net spendable income, is about as close as you will get.

The first step in evaluating a rental property is to determine the gross monthly rent. This may be done by checking various online resources such as Rentometer and Zillow. Another method is to call local property managers. Adam and I have been doing this for so long in our city that we know the rental rates in any neighborhood that we buy in. It is important to be as accurate as possible on the gross rents.

Step two is to determine all monthly expenses, including: vacancy, maintenance and reserves, real estate taxes, insurance, and management fees. I use about 5-7% of gross rent for vacancy and the same amount for maintenance and reserves. Most all of our properties are fresh, professional renovations, and in excellent condition, so our cost should be closer to the 5% range. You should adjust this rate to match your particular property. You can obtain the actual real estate tax from your local property appraiser. If the taxes seem particularly low, you may need to adjust up a bit as a new sale may trigger a tax increase. Also, make sure that if the property is homesteaded, you allow for loss of that exemption when the house becomes a rental property. Management fees in our market run about 10% of gross rent.

Once monthly expenses are estimated, simply subtract the monthly expenses from the scheduled gross rent and you will have the net monthly income. Multiply that amount by 12 to determine the net annual income.

Let's look at a sample rental property.

123 Cherry Road
Scheduled Monthly Rent: $800.00
Less:
Vacancy Factor (5%): $40.00
Maintenance & Reserves (5%): $40.00
Property Taxes: $70.00
Property Insurance: $60.00
Property Management (10%): $80.00
NET Spendable Monthly Income: $510.00
NET Spendable Annual Income: $6,120.00

The other factor that you need is the desired rate of return. I try to provide my turn-key buyers with a return rate around 12% (.12).

The final step is to divide the net annual income by the desired rate of return. $6,120.00/.12 = $51,000, which is the value of this property (based on $800 monthly rent and a 12% desired rate of return).

Please remember, never base the value of a rental property on any other factors than net income and desired rate of return. Follow this rule and you will never overpay. Break this rule by listening to someone else's opinion of value if you wish, but be prepared to live with the results.

Adam's Take on Determining Values

Joe has become an expert on valuing rental properties that will be used as investments. He uses his own approach to valuations, and it has been a very successful way for us to quickly analyze deals that we are considering for our clients as well as those we intend to purchase for our own personal portfolios. Many investors overcomplicate this process, and they like to pretend they are appraisers—or they want to talk about capitalization rates, which are commonly used to analyze apartments and multi-unit parcels. Joe's simple way of analyzing the cash on cash return from the market rent is the best way I have seen to analyze single family investment deals.

Valuing Retail Fix-and-Flip Properties

When I first joined Joe in the real estate business, I attended real estate school to become a licensed real estate agent. Back when I got my sales associate's license in Florida, there were no online schools, so I had to attend a local brokerage office to go through the class to learn what to study for my state exam. I was told to pay close attention to the section on valuations, so I took that advice and studied hard.

Thirty days after I got my real estate license, I got my first listing. My seller asked me to prepare a comparative market analysis, also known as a CMA. I searched the area his home was located in for comparable sales. Just like I learned in my real estate course, I was following the sales comparison approach to find similar sales. You simply search the neighborhood for homes most similar to the one you're listing, find what they sold for, and then use those comps to value your parcel.

While it sounds scientific and easy in theory, the sales comparison process can become quite daunting, and it can overwhelm many new agents and would-be real estate investors. The task of valuing homes by using the sales comparison approach is likely the most valuable component in structuring your retail-flip deal. While estimating the repairs is important, I see more bad deals out there due to the wrong value being attached than anything else. You need to be very careful when valuing your deals.

So, how do we quickly value properties? Well, the short answer is we track values in a small area first. Many investors will try to work deals all over their city based off of how good they think the deal is. They will focus on finding the deal, how much profit they want, and how much is needed for repairs, and then when a wholesaler posts the deal for sale, they will just trust the after-repair value given to them in the sales package. You should never do this. If you really want to get good at valuing properties to fix and flip in your area, I recommend getting your real estate license or teaming up with an experienced partner who can quickly estimate values. The reason I am stating this is due to the fact that you must have MLS access to get a true valuation.

Now, here's why this is so important: Your end goal is to sell the fix-and-flip deal to a home buyer. That home buyer is going to be getting a loan. Their lender will demand they get an appraisal. So, your estimated after-repair value had better be very close to that appraisal amount. The appraisers will only use MLS comps, so when you conduct your valuation, please make sure you only use the *recent sales* in the MLS. Below are the variables I use to value my fix-and-flip deals on MLS.

MLS specs to value retail fix-and-flip deals:

1. Comps must be within 1 square mile of your deal.
2. Comps must be like-kind properties. Use some common sense here. Is a 2-story, 2,500 SF brick home comparable to a 1-story 1,300 SF concrete block home? Most likely not, so do

not use this comp.

3. Comps must have sold in the last six months.
4. Comps must be of similar locations. If you have a water-front or a property with a premium view, you must make sure to use another premium comp.
5. Comps must be purchased by a retail buyer with a conventional, government, or financed loan. Do not use cash-purchased homes as comps since they are commonly bought at a discount.
6. Comps must not be bank foreclosures, short sales, or investor purchased. These homes are also bought at a discount.

The Sanity Test

It's very important when you're selecting comps that you use a sanity test. After you select a handful of comps, you need to follow this test.

First, I want you to print out the comps that you are planning to use and get a pen and notebook. Now, go out into the neighborhood and drive by the houses you are planning to use as comps. Make notes about each property and snap a photo of the outside. When you get back to your home or office, pull out the comps and place them on your desk or coffee table. Now, pull up a map and stare at the placement of each property while you read your notes and think about what it would be like to live at each house. You will find that some comps just aren't as good as your deal. Other properties will be too nice and should be discarded along with the inferior comps.

By staring at the map and the photos at the same time, you are training your brain and making mental notes of what each home is truly worth. I once printed out a huge map of the neighborhoods I was buying in and hung it on my wall. I then made notes about the type of houses on each street. My map revealed that there was a pocket of concrete block homes that a local builder constructed in the 1980s. They were well-built homes, but were worth much less than the homes two streets over that were 10 years newer and had a beautiful view of a neighborhood park. It was hard to feel the difference between the comps without actually driving around the neighborhood.

Ultimately, what I discovered was the pride of ownership was much higher just a few blocks over. I learned quickly to ignore those inferior comps that were close by, but were not worth as much as the better streets. You can get into real trouble by only staring at a map and spreadsheets. Get out there and view the comps. Once you learn the neighborhoods well, you can skip the car ride and get your offers in within minutes. It's important to start small and select neighborhoods that you understand.

A Simple Valuation Method to Value Retail Fix-and-Flip Deals

My formula for valuing deals is quite simple. I just select 3-5 good comps in the neighborhood, and then I find out what the price per square foot is for each home. After I get the price per square foot, I average it out. If I can't find three good comps, then I do not buy the deal as a fix and flip. If I can find at least three, then I take the average price per square foot and apply it to my deal.

Let's run through a quick and simple example. Please keep in mind we are pulling these numbers from Jacksonville, Florida's hot retail areas in 2017.

> *123 Main St.*
> *3 bedroom, 2 bath brick ranch home with basic upgrades*
> *1,500 SF*
> **Comp 1** *(like-kind property): 1,625 SF, sold for $178,750 in 35 days*
> *$178,750/1,625 = $110 per SF*

Comp 2 (like-kind property): 1,400 SF, sold for $168,000 in 17 days

$168,000/1,400 SF = $120 per SF

Comp 3 (like-kind property: 1,350 SF, sold for $157,950 in 42 days

$157,950/1,350 SF = $117 per SF

Average Price Per SF = 110+120+117 / 3 = $115.67

115.67 x 1,500 SF = $173,505

This simple method will allow you to quickly value your deals and get your offers submitted with lightning speed. If you require a more detailed estimate of value, then you will need to order a formal appraisal. Estimating accurate after-repair values on your fix-and-flip deals is partly artistic (when selecting the best comps) and partly scientific (when calculating the price per square foot). By developing local market knowledge, having MLS access, and gaining practice, you can become a retail fix-and-flip valuation superstar. You will become known as an expert who quickly recognizes the best deals and has the knowledge to put together solid valuations and profitable deals.

CHAPTER 10

Recognizing Profitable Deals

In the previous chapter, we discussed how to determine the value of a property. Just because the numbers work, however, is not the be-all and end-all of selecting a property. Adam and I have passed on many houses where the numbers pointed to a potential profit. Here are a few of the questions we always ask ourselves before buying a property.

How long will it take to turn the entire deal and get paid?

The length of time that a deal takes to complete will vary based on several factors, but it'll depend mostly on your method of disposition. If you are wholesaling the deal, you might be done in just a few weeks. If you are providing a renovated property to a landlord, expect three to four months. Moving a retail deal from acquisition to final payment is seldom accomplished in less than six months. If repairs are involved, the scope and complexity of the repairs are important factors to consider.

What assets will be tied up by doing this deal?

Two classes of assets will be used when turning a deal—*finite* and *infinite*. Examples of infinite assets are building materials, labor, and real estate agents. We may think there is a limited availability of these things, but believe me, these assets are everywhere and virtually unlimited. On the other hand, the best example of a finite asset is your time. A day only contains 24 hours, and there's not a single person on Earth who gets one second more. When it comes to money, we almost always feel it is finite, and we have only a certain amount available. That way of thinking can be overcome eventually, but when you are starting out, your cash on hand can be a limiting factor. For this reason, make sure you understand what assets will be tied up while doing a deal.

Could these assets be more profitably utilized elsewhere?
When considering a house deal involving substantial renovations, I want my profit to be roughly equal to my rehab costs. In other words, if I am considering spending $15,000 on renovations, I want to see about $15,000 gross profit in the deal. If I am going to flip the deal and not complete it myself, I will share that profit with my buyer. On a wholesale as-is flip, I am willing to accept a lower profit, but Adam and I have agreed on a minimum amount we will accept. If the profit is not there, we walk away from the deal.

For example, we recently considered a retail flip in the historic district. The numbers looked good, but having done other historic renovations, I knew that the process of dealing with the historic district rules and inspections can be tedious. In the final analysis, we determined that our assets (mainly our time) could be better utilized elsewhere. So we passed on the deal. We can earn similar profits—while putting in far less of our energy—by focusing on smaller and easier projects. In taking this path, our risk will be diversified and my life a bit less complicated. The lesson here is this: Just because you *can* do a deal does not mean you *should* do the deal.

Once repaired, will the property be one that I would want to own?
I have inspected a lot of houses that I would not take if they were

given to us for free. I use the term "inspected" loosely as my inspections consisted of opening the front door, walking around the interior, and quickly exiting the same way I entered. There does come a point where the only effective renovation tool is a bulldozer. The code that Adam and I use for this type of house is "BB" (bulldozer bait). Other houses may be salvageable but will always contain some flaws. Examples of this might be sagging but sound roof members, slightly leaning but stable walls, or other non-critical defects that just make the house less than desirable.

These houses sometimes sell to a low-end landlord, but more often than not, they're sold to an uneducated, newbie investor. This is because they are money pits. We don't buy, renovate, or sell these types of houses. I am going to be nice and not tell you what I think of people who market these types of properties to novice investors. One of our absolute rules is that we will not contract to purchase any home that we would not be comfortable owing in our personal portfolios. There is also a practical reason for this rule. My personal portfolio contains several houses that I put under contract and was unable to wholesale by the closing deadline. I always close, and if they don't sell quickly, I keep them myself. Again, I only buy houses that I am willing to keep.

Risk vs. Reward

This is the final hurdle. Consider the downside. I like to ask myself and my partner, Adam, "If we do this deal, what is the worst that could happen?" If we feel that the deal meets all of our criteria and the potential downside is something that we can accept and absorb, then we do the deal.

Perhaps the most important lesson real estate investors must learn is to balance risk and reward. Now, I am not a gambler. I have never even bought a lottery ticket. I would sooner flush a dollar down the toilet than to risk it trying to buy a dream—especially when my chance of success is one in millions. I could pitch pennies and have 50/50 odds. I have, however, made some pretty dumb real estate decisions. I have done a lot of studying, but most of my learning has been from the School of Hard Knocks. I hope you will learn from my mistakes and avoid the higher costs that I have paid. After many years, I believe I have finally overcome the lure of gambling or buying property in which the risks outweigh the potential rewards.

Shortly before the mortgage crisis, I decided that buying distressed properties was just too slow. The answer was to buy scattered lots and build new houses. The first two I built were sold before completion at a profit of around $22,000 each. This encouraged me to buy six more lots. I finished building these six houses right in the middle of the mortgage debacle. The values dropped by half. Before the crash, anybody with a pulse was qualifying for a home loan. Within a week, nobody was qualifying. In the end, I dumped these six houses for a bit more than *half* of their former value. That was a $500,000 seminar. As you can see, the School of Hard Knocks has expensive tuition!

Before the mortgage crisis, I thought that Florida real estate would appreciate forever. Now I realize that the stars in my eyes masked the potential risk. I did recover, but only after moving right back to buying distressed properties and doing what I knew how to do. With that said, let's take a look at the risk/reward balance of two popular real estate investing techniques—rentals and retail flips.

Rental Risks

1. Renovation costs could exceed budget.
2. It could take longer than anticipated to place a tenant.
3. Your taxes and insurance costs could increase.
4. Tenants could damage your property.

In all the above examples, the worst result is *decreased income.* Perhaps you bought the property expecting a 10% return but were only able to net 7%. Disappointing, yes. However, if you used your IRA money to fund this deal, which was most likely only earning 2-4%, then that's not exactly a disaster. You're still better off than you were before buying. I see this as a good risk vs. potential reward relationship. My entire retirement account is invested in residential rental property. I do not manage it, worry about it, or even drive by it. My property manager does all the daily work, and the net rent is deposited in my bank account monthly. To me, this is what being an investor is all about.

Retail Fix-and-Flip Risks

1. Renovation or building costs could exceed your budget.
2. Interest rates could rise, devaluing your house and slowing sales.
3. The market could take a dive, making your house basically unsellable, which means you'd need to rent it out. Flips are generally more expensive than rentals, so returns are much lower (see all the above rental risks).

These risks will result not only in a decrease or loss of profit, but you can actually *lose all or part of your investment.* If you have deep pockets, perhaps you can survive a lengthy market dip or crash, but even then, you will have valuable assets tied up. When markets crash, it is time to buy *not* sell. Having your money tied up in fix and flips can cost you a small fortune in missed opportunity. I believe that doing retail flips is NOT investing but is instead a simple retail business. I am not putting down the flippers; I am just stating that if you decide to go that route, you should know and be willing to accept the associated risks.

Again, risk vs. reward must always be considered when purchasing real estate property.

Adam's Take on Profitability

As I was sipping my coffee this morning, I began to brainstorm about my day. I always ask myself the same question every morning, just after finishing my morning routine. I look in the mirror and have a quiet talk with the guy staring back at me. "What are you going to do today, Adam, to earn a profitable income to feed your family?" As an entrepreneur, it's very important to ask yourself this question each day. I use this to motivate myself to focus on the paramount tasks ahead—those that need to be done first because they *directly* impact my income-earning abilities as a business owner.

I have found that focusing on what deals I am working on that month is the best place to start. There are many tasks—such as marketing, sales, developing and improving workflow systems, managing vendors and virtual assistants, conducting research and development, and a myriad of other responsibilities—that I tackle every week. These tasks directly support and help propel my company forward. With that being said, the task that directly impacts my bank account the most is doing actual deals. I figured this out a few years back when social media became a staple for marketing your small business. I ended up spending way too many hours during the week posting updates and too little time working on my deals. Needless to say, I went broke for a few months.

While I did gain some followers on my social threads, my bank accounts suffered immeasurably, and I ended up paying our bills for a few months with high-interest credit cards. This was not a great place to be as a small business owner and a father with young kids. In order to succeed with a real estate investing company, you need to focus on your deals. To get a better understanding of how to do deals successfully, let's run through a few examples. These are actual deals that Joe and I have recently completed.

While you're reading about these deals, I want you to think long and hard about how we are discovering the hidden profit inside of each deal. It's not always so apparent. If you can learn how to sniff out profit in real estate deals, you will never have to work another day locked inside of a cubicle. Instead, you'll be able to earn six figures a year while working 25-30 hours a week. Now, let's jump right in!

The Deal on 1322 Wolfe Street

I didn't really find this deal; it found me. I stay pretty active in my local business community and I network often. At a local networking event in Jacksonville, I was approached by a gentleman who had just bought a national real estate investor company as a franchise. I was astonished to find out how much he'd paid to purchase his franchise and what he was spending each month on advertising to dig up good deals on houses. He'd spent a pretty penny that month, and he had a couple of deals that he wanted me to look up. However, he didn't actually have much of a buyers list yet, and he needed to sell some properties to keep his business going. He asked if he could email me some deals, so I gave him my business card and told him to send me what he had. Long story short, I spent a day looking at his deals and we actually ended up buying one of them.

Can you tell me about the deal, Adam?

1322 Wolfe Street
1,444 SF
2 bedroom / 2 bath concrete block home in a historic area of Jacksonville, Florida.
The home has a very basic layout and is on a 50ft lot.

How did I unlock the hidden profit inside the deal?

I quickly identified this home as being located in a very hot retail area. The average number of days that homes take to sell in this neighborhood is 15 days. This told me that if we priced this home right at market value, and if we renovated the home to look like the comparable homes that had sold, we could sell it very quickly.

The investor who wanted to sell me the deal believed the home would need $30,000 or more in repairs to get the property in good and saleable condition. When we got inside, we estimated the repairs at only $9,250. Now, this investor did a good job at estimating the after-repair value, which he said would be $260,000-$270,000, but he was way off on the repair estimate. By knowing the correct repair estimate, we were immediately able to grab $20,750 in profit on the deal upfront. In the end, we contracted to purchase the deal on Wolfe Street for $185,000.

How did I structure the deal to get the profit in my pocket quickly?

I knew I had the deal under contract at $185,000, plus the repairs needed of $9,250, so my total amount in the deal was $194,250. I also accounted for the soft costs of getting the deal done, and put this at around 8% of the after repair value, or another $20,000. So, the total amount invested would be $214,250.

As you can see, with the after-repair value being in the $260,000-$270,000 range, there was still plenty of profit in this deal. According to our calculations, we could expect to profit around $45,000-$55,000. We knew that we could take six months and do this deal ourselves, but we decided to wholesale it and take a $15,000 mark up. It only took us a week to earn that $15K, and we took on virtually zero risk. In six months, we could do 25 deals like this and earn $375K instead of $55K. In reality, it would be hard to get that many good deals, but I think you can see the lesson here. You can earn way more money by packaging up deals like this and wholesaling them. There's nearly an endless number of investors who want to fix and flip homes. The key to your success is sniffing the profit out of each and every deal.

The Deal on 6231 Elise Street

I found this deal after receiving a phone call from a buddy I went to high school with. During the last few years, we'd been playing softball together and attending the same church. He told me that his dad was thinking about selling a home that he owned. Joe and I visited the house and submitted an offer. My friend's dad told us the offer was too low and he wanted to negotiate. We simply told him that was the most we could pay and we wished him good luck. He ended up renting out the house to a family member, but called us back six months later. He told us he would take less than we had originally offered. We asked, "Why would you want us to purchase it for less?" It turned out that his wife had gotten sick and the family now desperately needed some quick cash to pay for medical bills. In the end, we offered to pay our original amount and closed three weeks later.

Can you tell me about the deal, Adam?

6231 Elise Drive
1,150 SF
3 bedroom / 1.5 bath concrete block home in a middle-class neighborhood in Jacksonville, Florida.
The home has a very basic layout and is on a 75ft lot.

How did I unlock the hidden profit inside the deal?

We ran comps on this house and estimated its after-repair value at $115,000. The home had very basic fixtures and no upgrades, so we knew we would have to spend some money to modernize the home and make it first-time-homebuyer ready. We placed the deal under contract for $54,000, and the home needed around $20,000 in upgrades to renovate it to retail-flip standards—with granite counters and an all-new kitchen. We made our money when we bought this one. If you can buy good properties for 50% of value or less, it's really hard to lose. Just make sure you inspect them properly, that they have a sound structure—and that they're not sitting on any environmental hazards or something similar—and you will be in great shape.

How did I structure the deal to get the profit in my pocket quickly?

I knew this deal was living in the gray area. Was it a fix-and-flip retail deal, or a buy-and-hold rental? I ran some comps and discovered that the average time to sell this home would be around 30 days if we priced it at market value. I calculated that I could earn around $25,000-$30,000 in profit if I did the fix and flip myself. I then analyzed the deal as a buy-and-hold rental. I learned that an investor could rent the unit out for $1,000 per month. His net return on his all-cash investment would be 10% after all expenses were paid, and he would only need to spend $9,330 on renovations to get the unit rent ready. I immediately picked up the phone and called an investor in California that I had been working with. Dave purchased that property from me for $71,000, and we closed three days later. As you can see, it only took Joe and me four days to earn $17,000 in profit. How's that for risk vs. reward? Dave was stoked because he's earning a great return on his money, and he's sitting on $30,000 in equity. This deal was a win for all parties involved. The seller got to pay his wife's medical bills, Dave got to put his money to work, and Joe and I earned an income. As we've said before, always figure out a way to put together win-win deals.

The Deal on 3142 Mecca Street

We found this deal from the MLS. It was a bank foreclosure being sold by Veterans Affairs. We got inside the property the day it was listed, and we submitted our offer along with 30 other offers that hit the listing agent's desk that day. The home was beat up inside and had what looked like mold on the walls. The bank called for highest and best and refused to acknowledge anyone's offer unless they signed a Hold Harmless Agreement. I submitted our notarized and witnessed agreement that stated we would hold the bank harmless of any mold that may exist in the property. I got the document over to them within the hour.

An hour later, they accepted our offer. By the time they accepted our offer, a total of 62 offers had come into the broker's office. We were able to get this deal under contract by exerting absolute speed! We saw the property for what it was, inspected the property in the field, executed a document immediately, and agreed to no inspection period with cash to close in 14 days. This is a perfect example of expertise, speed, and execution at work. In this case, we were the perfect buyer for purchasing a distressed property from the bank.

Can you tell me about the deal, Adam?

3142 Mecca Street
1,142 SF
3 bedroom / 1.5 bath concrete block home in a low-income neighborhood.
This home was on a cul-de-sac and had two separate living areas, a large laundry room, and a large eat-in kitchen. This home is a rental only.

How did I unlock the hidden profit inside the deal?

This home looked way worse than it was. The mold everyone was so frightened by washed right off with a garden hose. How do we know this? We brought water with us and sprayed it on the wall. Now, do you think outside of the box like that when you're viewing bank foreclosures? Probably not. Most investors are too scared to do stuff like this, but you should. I can tell you that we did have an EPA-certified general contractor named Joe on our team who took a look at it. Joe ensured us that the home was in great shape and would be a great rental to add to any investor's portfolio. We also discovered that the home could be converted into a 4 bedroom, which would increase the monthly rent and our cash flow. So, we purchased the home for pennies on the dollar.

How did I structure the deal to get the profit in my pocket quickly?

This deal fits right into our turn-key renovation deals. We sold the deal 24 hours later to one of our repeat customers who will earn a healthy return on their money. We bought the deal for $18,450 and then resold it for $43,000. At closing, we earned $24,550 on this deal. We will be renovating this one for our client, and although it will take us 60 days to finish the work, we will get paid as a contractor during the renovations. Once again, all parties are happy. The bank got a distressed property with possible mold liability issues off their books, our investor got a healthy return on their retirement funds, and Joe and I got a fat paycheck.

The Vacant Land Deal on 0 Fort Caroline Road

We found this deal from attempting to buy a large house that was listed by the bank and sold by an online real estate auction company. When we visited the large, beat-up home, we noticed that it had a very large lot, so we analyzed the parcel size on the tax assessor website. By viewing the parcel map online, we discovered that the parcel only included one lot and that the half-acre lot next door was on a separate parcel tax identification number, and it wouldn't be included in the bank sale. So, we sent a letter to the owner who lived out of state, and he called us back a week or so later. We found out he was actually the son of the owner and that his dad was out sailing and wouldn't be on shore for a few more weeks. So, while we waited, we placed our highest bid for the main house at the auction, and we were grossly outbid.

We did some further investigating and found out that the pool that was attached to the large home for sale was encroaching on the vacant lot. We finally heard from the father who owned the vacant parcel, and he told us he was willing to sell, but that the bank knew about the pool encroachment and was refusing to do anything about it. The home had sat vacant for seven years, and during that time, he felt his vacant property had lost value and was not worth much anymore.

Can you tell me about the deal, Adam?

0 Fort Caroline Road, 32225
One half-acre cleared vacant lot
Located in an upper middle-class zip code

How did I unlock the hidden profit inside the deal?

We contracted to buy the vacant lot for $6,500. We agreed to sign an agreement stating that we were aware of the pool encroachment and that we would take the parcel as-is. The surrounding homes next to this half acre were selling for $300,000 to $400,000, and the lot was located just down the road from an Arnold Palmer-designed golf course and country club. This lot happened to be one of the last available parcels to build on in the area, and it was twice as large as anything available in the neighborhood.

So, we had the problem of dealing with the pool encroachment.

We soon figured out how to solve the problem. We ordered a new land survey and carved out the portion of the lot that does not touch the pool. We created two separate parcels with two separate deeds. By doing so, we were able to allow a home buyer to purchase the vacant lot and build a new home without worrying about having a cloud on the title or an encroachment. Our plan is to sell them both parcels separately so they can build their home and then sell the pool-encroached parcel to the new owner later. Whatever they decide to do, it's a great lot where they can build their dream home. Builders are in the area developing the last sought-after parcels, so it won't be hard to sell.

How did I structure the deal to get the profit in my pocket quickly?

As you may have guessed, this is an ongoing deal. At the time of this writing, the market value for this vacant parcel is around $89,000. I purchased and sold a lesser parcel down the road that was not cleared for $69,000, and it only took me 25 days to get a contract. So, if all goes well, we stand to net $82,500 on this vacant land deal. We had to do some creative things to track down the owner, get him to agree to sell to us for cheap, and then fix the parcel with a new survey, but, as you can see, this will be a wildly successful deal.

Did you notice that every deal involved a different situation? Many times, investors will posture and act like they are bigger than the deals they do. They will purchase luxury cars, wear expensive suits, talk fast, move too quickly, and treat people like dirt. They rarely listen to what the seller is trying to tell them. The fact is, every deal that you buy will have a story. You need to ask yourself the following question: If the seller could list this home with a real estate agent and be paid a fair price, why wouldn't they just do that? The truth is, people are not dumb. If they can list with a local agent, pay them a commission, and sell the property quickly for a fair price, that's exactly what they will do. You should always ask the seller *why* they are selling.

So, every deal has a story. I like to tell people that I do not buy houses, I buy stories. Learning those stories and developing a solution for the seller's problem is the secret to doing profitable deals. As you can see from the example deals we just shared, the best deals will show up *after* you develop a reputation for being a buyer who's reliable and can solve people's problems.

Every marketing piece that you send to a motivated seller should tell them that you are a serious buyer who can solve their problem. Divorcing couples have a problem—their life is a wreck, and the judge is forcing them to sell. Heirs who live in a different city have a problem—they inherited a beat-up property that keeps getting flagged by the city for code violations. Investors who purchased when the market was hot have a problem—they paid too much for the property and are emotionally spent. There are many other problems out there worth solving. If you can identify properties with value inside the deal and communicate to the seller that you are a problem-solver—and then package up the deal to sell—you will very easily earn enough income to be highly successful in this business for years to come.

CHAPTER 11

Managing Renovations

At the age of 21, after completing 75% of my degree in architecture and building construction technology, I left college to take a job with the City of Jacksonville. I worked with the city's Engineering Department for seven years and left as an assistant engineer. I have been a Florida state certified general contractor since 1988 and earned my state-certified roofing license in 2002. My experience with renovating residential houses began in 1982. Now, many years later, and with over 400 renovations under my belt, I do consider myself to be an expert in this arena.

While construction education and certifications are helpful, they do not totally prepare you for renovating houses. The bulk of my renovation education has been gleaned from making mistakes, learning how to fix them, and, of course, paying the price. This is what I like to call the School of Hard Knocks, and it is the world's most prolific educator. I hope you will not be as hard-headed as I was. Seems I had to make the same mistakes two or three times before finally learning to avoid them. Hopefully, you will be able to learn from my mistakes and only make a few of your own. The fact is, however, no education can duplicate the experience of making and paying for your own mistakes. That is how we truly learn.

With that said, it is not possible for me to impart all the necessary contracting skills in one chapter of a book. I can, however, give you some basic information about renovating residential properties.

Before we jump into a remodeling project, think back to Chapter 1 when you analyzed your assets and abilities. If a mechanical aptitude and construction experience are not among your abilities, you should strongly consider hiring a professional contractor to renovate your houses. But regardless of whether you decide to manage renovations yourself or hire a contractor, you will need some basic renovation knowledge.

A common thread within the real estate business is to work in reverse—sell it before you buy it, decide the final use before determining value, etc. Renovation is no different as the desired end-use of the property will strongly determine how the renovation is done. Step one, therefore, is to decide if the final disposition of the property will be a retail flip or a portfolio rental. Let's begin with remodeling a property that will be resold to an owner occupant.

The great country music star Kenny Rogers was right when he wrote, "You gotta know when to hold 'em and know when to fold 'em." The first order of business is to make sure that the house you're considering is worth renovating. In Chapter 15, we will talk about profit gremlins, but for now, I just want to mention a couple of the more obvious "gremlins" to look for when considering a renovation.

When I first approach a property, I always look at the roof. Sagging roofs can be very expensive to repair and will most always require a building permit. If the roof is composed of pre-engineered trusses, an engineer will need to certify the repair plan. Although I am capable and qualified to do structural work, I shy away from swaying and sagging truss roofs. It's just not worth it.

Another thing to look out for are foundation cracks. These may range from barely visible hairline cracks to separations wide enough to stick your fist in. Any crack wider than a pencil lead could present a problem. The same can be said about cracks in walls. Unless you're an engineer or an experienced contractor, you are going to need some expert assistance to analyze cracks in foundations and walls. As a rule of thumb, moderate foundation cracks (up to half an inch or so) that have moved laterally (horizontally) but not in shear (vertical displacement) are simple to repair. But, before repairing larger cracks, the cause of the cracking must first be determined, and this again will require investigation by an expert.

I recently viewed a house next to the boat ramp in my neighborhood that was on a beautiful riverfront lot. It was potentially worth up to a half million dollars, but I only offered $60,000. Somebody outbid me, paid $160,000, and moved in shortly thereafter. The house was built on a lot steeply sloped down to the riverbank. Erosion from rainwater drainage had seriously undermined the foundation. One of the third-story bedrooms was tilting four inches wall-to-wall, and there was a one-inch-wide crack in the load-bearing wall in the lower-level family room. This cracked wall was supporting a distributed load from two stories above. Had my bid been accepted, my plan was to tear down the existing home and sell the bare lot only. Last week, while launching my boat, I noticed the property had a fresh new dock and boathouse (probably a $50K expenditure). The foundation issues had not been touched. I wouldn't spend a single night in this house. In most cases, and especially as a beginning investor, you need to not only walk but *run* from houses containing serious structural flaws.

Basic Renovation Management Concepts

Let's go over the first three steps in the renovation process: plan, plan, and plan some more! Without proper planning, you will spend much more time and money to accomplish less. A detailed scope of work is the foundation of any great renovation plan.

To clarify, a scope of work is a simple list of items to be completed. I like to keep each work item description to seven or eight words.

This allows me to place the items on an Excel spreadsheet where I can later add values. This allows for one document that will serve as both the scope of work *and* the renovation estimate.

Now, there are three categories of items you will need to consider: labor, materials, and subcontractors. Every renovation item will fit into one or more of these categories. The breakdown within these categories will describe how you wish to accomplish the work for each item. For example, let's consider painting. You can hire a sub-contractor who will furnish all labor and materials to complete the painting work for a fixed price. In this case, you would enter only the total price under the "Subcontractor" column.

Let's assume you prefer to pay workers hourly, and you furnish the materials yourself. You would then enter estimated hours, pay rate, and materials in the appropriate columns. Perhaps you want to go the labor and materials route on the walls, but would prefer to hire a subcontractor to paint the ceilings at a fixed price. This would be represented in all three categories. It really is this simple to build an adequate scope of work and estimate. What I just described is exactly what I do. Once completed, the scope/estimate is provided to the renovation crew leader to accomplish the work. Prior to beginning the work, I meet my renovator on the job to discuss the work items and answer any questions.

Now, I am going to give you an ironclad rule: *Never pay for any work that is not complete.* For most of you, it is not a question of whether you will violate this rule, but when—and how much break-ing this rule will cost you. About 30 years ago, I learned this lesson at the School of Hard Knocks. Tuition for this particular lesson was $3,500. While on my way out of town to fish in a bass tournament, I had to meet with a roofing contractor on a rehab job. I was in a hurry to get on my way, and I had used these roofers in the past. I'd found them to be honest and reliable. They even had a Bible study at lunch and the name of their company was "Christian Roofing." I broke my own rule and gave them a $3,500 advance to buy materials. That was the last time I ever saw them. Now, as a Christian myself, I have forgiven them, but I will never again pay anyone in advance. How much will it cost you to learn this lesson?

Managing Renovation for a Retail Flip

When renovating a property for a retail flip, your number one priority should be making the property sellable. No matter how great a renovation you do, if the property is not easy to sell, you have failed. So, set your personal preferences aside and learn to concentrate on those factors that are imperative to salability. The first thing that a potential buyer sees is the exterior. This sight will be ingrained in their memory, and this mental image will set their expectations and greatly affect their attitude towards the property. If you have ever studied salesmanship, you understand that consumer buying decisions are seldom based on logic. Emotion is usually the overriding factor when making a major purchase.

I remember back when I was a young draftsman working for the city. I didn't make a lot of money at that job, so I began to buy and sell used cars to supplement my income. Now, I was not an expert on cars, but I had studied sales and understood why people buy—emotion! I would look for cars that were in average mechanical condition, but were really dirty and neglected. I would buy them cheap and do a fantastic cleaning, waxing, and detailing job. I sold them quickly, because when buyers showed up, their first impression was very positive and their mind told them, "Anybody who would keep a car this clean and shiny would have certainly maintained it well." When it comes to sales, emotion is king!

Likewise, the exterior of a retail flip must be beautiful and the yard landscaped nearly to perfection. Now, I do understand that a $150,000 home does not demand the same level of landscaping as a $500,000 home, but do not skimp here. The exterior will set the expectation for prospective buyers, and if they do not like the outside, they will never come inside. If the exterior is painted, use lighter colors and save strong, darker colors for accents like the entry door and shutters. Two of the most important features to consider in a retail renovation are kitchens and baths. The cabinets should be good quality and counters should be solid surface or granite. We always tile the splash area all the way up to the bottom of the cabinets. Most buyers are looking for stainless appliances. In the baths, we either replace or refinish the bathtub. Unless it is attractive and in great condition, the floor and tub tile should be replaced. We replace almost all vanities and prefer the "furniture look" vanities that come preassembled.

Interior walls should be light colored. We prefer light beige or light sage green. If you can afford it, install hard tile or quality vinyl flooring in lighter tones. If carpet is installed, stay with lighter colors. The key word is "neutral." Avoid strong colors on main components. Styles will change with the times, so use bright stylish colors and patterns as accents only. Your buyers will want to personalize the home themselves, so forget what you like and stick with the basics.

Managing Renovation for a Rental Property

When renovating a property to be used as a rental, your number one priority should be making the property functional and durable. The home should be nice enough to attract a tenant; however, it does not have to rise to the level of a retail flip.

Cleanliness, however, should never be compromised. A clean home attracts a clean tenant. Clean tenants tend to be better tenants, so hire a professional cleaner to prep for occupancy. We always install new mini-blinds and shower curtains. When the budget allows, we avoid carpeting and install hard flooring. If the home has wood flooring that can be refinished, that is a positive factor. The useful life of tile, heavy vinyl strip flooring, and refinished wood is much longer than carpeting. Over a 10-year period, the more durable floors will actually cost less than carpeting. If your budget is tight, I would consider carpeting for bedrooms only.

Most of the time, we can save the kitchen cabinets. We do any needed repairs, and, if they are ugly, we paint them with a bright white enamel and add contemporary brushed nickel hardware. Unless the countertops are nice, we typically replace them with new plastic laminate tops. Most of the time we tile the backsplash area for durability. Same with the baths. We save what we can and replace what we can't save. If the bathtub is rough but solid, we have it refinished. If the tile around the tub is deteriorated beyond repair, we rip it out along with the drywall behind it and install new backing and tile. If the tile is solid but ugly, we have our refinisher prep and spray it along with the tub. Don't spend a lot of time repairing toilets and vanities. They're cheap, so just remove and replace them.

The exterior of the home needs to be clean with no rotten wood or peeling paint. We often paint the eaves a dark color, especially if the wood is worn and needs caulking. Dark colors hide imperfections while light colored eaves display every crack and flaw. Unless the base exterior colors are hideous, stick with them. If you have to repaint, use a light- to medium-tone neutral main color, with bright decorator colors on doors and shutters. The driveway should be well defined, and a mulched planting bed created near the front of the house. Fences should be in good repair. If the house is frame construction and your budget allows, installing vinyl eaves and siding is a big plus. Vinyl looks great, is extremely durable, and, if you use light colors, it will never fade or need painting.

Again, there is no way I can make you a renovation expert, or even give you all the tools you will need in one short chapter. With that said, my goal is to familiarize you with the overall process to help you make more informed decisions.

Adam's Take on Renovating

For this chapter, I am going to assume you know nothing about renovations and that you're hiring a contractor. I do not have the engineering background that Joe does, and I am only slightly handy around my own house. To be completely honest, I know very little about actual construction. The best part is you don't need to be a contractor or know all that much to get your deals renovated. We titled this chapter "Managing Renovations" for a reason.

Even if you are a contractor or extremely handy, I believe you will earn the highest profit on your real estate investment deals by *not* doing the physical work yourself. Instead, I recommend hiring someone else to do it. Your time will be better spent managing the renovation rather than swinging the actual hammer.

How to Find Vendors

I was lucky enough to grow up around the renovation business watching my dad run the crews. One of the things that I learned from a young age was that the industry seemed to be flooded with guys who would fake like they knew more than they did. When he asked them if they could hang drywall, they would always say they were the best. If he asked them how good they were with electrical, they would immediately tell him they knew all about it. So, how do you tell who is going to charge a fair price for good work and who isn't? Well, it's really not that hard if you follow our basic formula for successfully hiring your renovation subcontractors.

The Basic Formula for Hiring Quality Subcontractors

1. Join your local real estate investor club.
2. Talk to other investors about what areas you are buying in and what type of renovations you want to start doing.
3. Build a list of trusted and verified subcontractors for every aspect of the renovation.

You really should not spend your time trying to scout hidden talent in the renovation field. I always seem to meet the same guy at real estate investor meetings who says he is good at finding labor. Someone will ask if anyone has a good electrician, and he will raise his hand and say that he has a guy. Actually, he seems to have a guy for everything. Do you need a roofer? He has a guy. Do you need a plumber? He has a guy. He has a ton of vendors and he doesn't mind sharing. So, this guy is a gold mine for locating quality vendors. Find this guy at your local real estate investor club meeting, grab a paper and pen, and write down all his vendors. Some groups even have preferred vendors that they use who regularly work with investors. Not every vendor will be a perfect match, so you'll need to use them on a deal first to see if they're a good fit.

One of the helpful real estate investors I spoke to actually admitted that he finds all his vendors at the local Home Depot. He ventures down there at the crack of dawn and finds all the renovation guys when they're picking up their materials. His theory is that the sub-contractors who are bums can't seem to wake up early enough to get anything done, while the ones who get there early usually do quality work. If you are hands-on, you can try this tactic. However, you won't catch me down there. I would rather build my vendor list at our local meetings and let this guy run to the hardware store.

How to Estimate Repairs

A few years ago, we realized our mentoring students were having a hard time estimating repairs for their deals. We wanted to help, so we developed an easy spreadsheet where they can input how much each item would cost to repair. We then took them all out on a bus tour and let them input how much it would cost to replace all the doors on a house, how much an entire rewiring would cost, how much to replace the roof, and more.

As Joe mentioned earlier, the spreadsheet was broken down into labor + materials + subcontractor costs. If you hire an hourly guy to paint the walls, but you provide the paint, then you add up the costs of the paint plus how long it takes him to paint the home. If you hire a painting crew to come in and paint the entire home for a fixed fee, and they bring the materials, then you just punch in the full costs of the subcontractor. This works for electrical, plumbing, kitchens, baths, and anything else.

If you do not want to get involved at all, you could just hire a general contractor to do all the work for you. So, how do you figure out what the doors cost, what the paint costs, etc.? Well, that one is easy. Just open up Microsoft Excel and start a spreadsheet for all the major categories of the renovation. Once you get down roofing, plumbing, electrical, paint, flooring, cabinets, countertops, appliances, lighting fixtures, siding, windows, doors, HVAC, and the water heater, you will have most of the major components carved out. Now, you need to head down to your local Home Depot and get cost estimates for each component. You may also need to go to some larger building suppliers to get quotes on the roofing shingles, windows, and HVAC.

When it comes time to estimate the smaller stuff like hardware, trims, light bulbs, and such, just add some new rows to the spreadsheet, and you can get prices for those. Now, you can go out and shop the prices and try to find the best deals. But, once again, if you attend a local real estate investor meeting, there will be hands-on renovators who can tell you where to find the best prices on materials. Now that you know what labor and materials are going to cost, you can go out and get turn-key pricing from subcontractors. Just call up the roofer, the plumber, and the turn-key home remodeling company, and get quotes from them. By knowing what the materials and labor costs are, you should be able to identify their markup and make sure you are not getting ripped off. You can get super involved in the project if you like, but a guy who loves building systems like myself will always tell you to understand what you are paying for, but hire someone else to do the work.

My goal has always been to know how to talk to the roofer and make sure I am getting a good price. All I need to know is that he's doing a good job; I don't need to do the actual roofing myself. Each scenario and project is different, but developing a system for tracking materials, labor, and subcontractors is your best bet for effectively renovating your deal for maximum profit.

How to Maximize Profit

As you can see, I will always recommend that you hire someone else to do the renovation work for you. I truly believe that in order to scale your investment business, your time will be better spent on marketing, sales, personnel, and investment analysis. You can achieve great success managing the renovation on your deal, but please promise me you will not get bogged down by picking up the power drill and hanging the actual drywall.

I want to wrap up this chapter by telling you the story of a guy I know who was very hands-on with his renovations. When I met Chris, he was working on his second investment deal. He admitted to me that he hadn't earned a dime from his first fix and flip, but that he did get it sold, and he was able to get his cash back for this second deal. Chris loved to visit his local hardware store and check out the new products for the quarter. He loved talking about what lighting fixtures worked well for a middle-class house and what new flooring was hot with first-time home buyers. He spent countless hours designing the layout of the kitchen, and he actually got pretty good using CAD and some other software to design spaces within the home.

I loved his renovations and he had a knack for finding good labor at a fair price. He learned how to buy materials in bulk from suppliers, and he eventually bought a small metal warehouse to house the materials, which he placed at the back of his half-acre property. He also learned how to pull permits for windows, roofs, electrical, and plumbing, and had gotten friendly with the local municipal building inspectors. For all intents and purposes, Chris was doing extremely well as a renovator. So, why wasn't he making any money?

The truth is, Chris had learned how to become a *renovator*—not an investor. An investor understands how to manage his time, and he also understands that he must be frugal on some products and may not always need to replace everything in the home. Investors also spend most of their time structuring the deal and staring at their bottom-line profit. They are always worried about value and salability, market timing, and finishing the project quickly.

Chris was not an investor. He fell in love with doing the renovations. Eventually, he got his contractor's license and began doing work for other investors like myself. Do not become like Chris if you want to maximize your profits. Focus on finding and structuring profitable deals, manage your renovations from a distance, and stay away from the hammer. By following this formula for success, you will be able to maximize your profit for every deal.

CHAPTER 12

Funding Your Deals

Finding the money to do real estate deals is not the critical path to success. Finding good deals is much more difficult than finding money. After 30+ years in the business, I cannot remember a period when lack of money held me back. I can remember being poor, but I have never lacked access to money. Regardless of what the gurus advertise, you *do* need money to buy real estate.

To find that money, just ask yourself a simple question…

Who's Got the Money?

Back in the depression, Will Rogers was hired by the federal government to push the WPA program. This program was developed to create jobs and help Americans get out of the soup lines and back to work. Will was giving a speech, talking about all the ditches, dams, and bridges that would be repaired and built, when a skeptical man in the crowd asked loudly, "That is all well and good, but where's all this money coming from?" Will cocked and scratched his head before answering, "Well, I reckon from them that's got it." Will nailed it! To this day, there is no other place to find money. With that in mind, here are a few places to look:

1. **Do you have the money?** If you have money in the bank or in a retirement plan, and you're not depending on it for emergencies or living expenses, this money will be the

least expensive and safest funding available. Many of our cash buyers fund the transaction with their private IRAs.

It is a simple process to convert most retirement plans to self-directed status. If you do this, your IRA will actually own the real estate and, of course, you will own the IRA. America's oldest and most trusted self-directed IRA custodian is Equity Trust Corporation. Just google their name for a wealth of information.

2. **Do your relatives or friends have the money?** The IRAs of the Baby Boomers alone exceeds 30 trillion dollars, and the majority of that money is earning less than 5%. This is where I've found the majority of the money I have used to build my personal portfolio. Years ago, I developed a program that I call my "984 Loan Program."

984 Loan Program

The 984 Loan Program is based on my willingness to borrow money at 9% interest over 84 months. I learned that I could borrow $23,000 on a house that rented for $700 monthly. After paying all expenses and the mortgage, I would still have a positive monthly cash flow between $100 and $150. Not even I can buy many houses that I can be "all in" at $23,000. I could, however, dig up a few houses that I could buy in as-is condition for under $23,000. I would borrow the $23,000 to buy the house and then do the repairs with my own funds. My total investment averaged approximately $10,000 per house. My tenants paid off the 984 loan over my first seven years of ownership. My return on investment was over 18% on the $10,000, and after 84 months, the property was mine, free and clear. I used this method to get started. It was a lot of work and effort, but well worth it to build a nice retirement.

My first ten rental properties utilizing this program provided me with a spendable monthly income of about $5,000. I will receive this income for the remainder of my life, and it will adjust with inflation. Due to the depreciation write-off, I will pay minimal income taxes. When my wife and I are gone, our three sons will receive the income. Utilizing a family trust and professional property manager, these are true sustainable, hands-off investments. The real beauty of this is I did not invest the $23,000 per house. I borrowed it and my tenants were nice enough to pay it back for me. My lenders made 9%, I built a great retirement income and an estate to leave my heirs, and the contractors made a living rehabbing my houses. My property manager gets profitable business, and my tenants get a great home to live in. That's a win-win-win-win-win. What a wonderful country!

I will continue to build my portfolio for at least ten more years, but due to the growth and success of our business, I now have a bit more cash to invest. If you have time to locate, repair, and buy property directly from sellers, but not a lot of cash, the 984 Loan Program is a great way to begin building your rental portfolio.

I do want to make sure you understand that if you have available funds, use your own money first. The 984 Program is where my long-term buy and hold strategy began. On the first 10 houses that I financed, I only owe a total of $41,000. Every time I get a few extra bucks, I pay one off. I have never actually gone the full 84 months, and I have other houses that I never borrowed against. Don't be afraid to change the parameters and develop your own private money system. I found 984 to be my sweet spot, but on my last financed house, I only did 36 months. Also, unless you are a full-time real estate entrepreneur with a talent for finding wholesale deals, your per-house investment may exceed the amount where you can safely service the debt. If you have a good job but not a lot of cash, I would suggest keeping your job for a while as you slowly begin to build your portfolio with private financing.

Do Banks Have the Money?

Yes, they do—but on their terms, not yours. I had an associate and friend who really believed in working with banks. He had a line of credit up to about half a million dollars. He would borrow on his credit line at 6%, lend the money to other investors at 15%, and pocket the spread. He made great money until the mortgage crash. Right after the crash, the bank called his line of credit due. The money, however, was invested in homes that lost half of their value. His borrowers could not pay him back, and he could not pay the bank. The next time I saw him, he had declared Chapter 11 bankruptcy and his new BMW had become an old pickup truck. My buddy eventually recovered and went back to being a real estate agent.

My advice is to use banks for checking, but not for borrowing. Their terms are absolutely in their own interest. You should always use your own cash when available as this money will be available at the lowest cost and risk. Don't use money you need for living expenses or emergency funds, but long-term savings and retirement funds are an excellent source. Next, look to the same sources from friends and relatives (using a 984 Loan Program). If you are doing a retail flip, look for a funding partner and split the profits. Borrowing excessively from institutional lenders is like owning a pet alligator. You feed it everything you can (extra savings, investment funds, and cash flow) in hopes that it will eat you last.

Attracting Private Financing

I once had a student named Dan. He was a successful building contractor who purchased several homes from me over a couple of years. I taught a class on private financing that Dan was attending for the second time. After the class, he approached me and said, "I can't find anyone who will give me financing." I answered, "How many people have you asked?" After four or five mumbled half-answers and avoidances, Dan finally gave me the answer: "None." He had casually mentioned his real estate investing to others and was expecting them to ask if they could lend him money. The truth was that, being a sharp and successful guy, Dan wasn't comfortable asking to borrow money from others.

Here is my basic script for soliciting private 984 loans: "Do you have any money in savings or a retirement plan that is not safely and consistently earning you 9%?" If the answer is yes, I tell them the story of another lender who is funding houses for me. By the time I've finished, I almost always have a commitment. The Book of James states, "Ye have not, because ye ask not." You need to ask! Once you break the ice with a couple of private lenders, and after you've repaid them on time, you will be approached by their friends and relatives offering to lend you investment capital. It really is that easy. At this point in our business, Adam and I never worry about funding. Funding for us is always as close as an email or phone call.

Again, finding the money to do real estate deals is not the critical path to real estate investing success. Learn to find great and profitable deals, overcome your fear and pride, and ask everyone you know, and I promise you the money will come.

Adam's Take on Funding

Finding funding for your deals is as easy as cake. You can find funding, and you can find it now. Did you know that as of December 31st, 2016, the total amount of retirement assets in America was 25.3 trillion dollars? 25 trillion dollars, man! That's a whole lot of cheddar. I meet investors all the time who tell me there just isn't any money out there for investors who want to do fix-and-flip deals. They say there just isn't any money for an investor who wants to own cash-producing rental property. Well, I think the statistics speak for themselves. There is plenty of money out there to fund every deal you do. You just need to learn how to get access to it.

For some reason, this seems to be the hardest part for many investors. Why are we all so afraid to ask people to use their money? I believe there are a few common reasons why investors are unable to attract funding:

1. **We lack confidence.** We are just absolutely terrified of letting people down. Our fear of not being able to repay the money keeps us from asking anyone to borrow it.

2. **Public speaking scares us.** Public speaking has been identified as one of the top fears among consumers. If you can overcome your fear of public speaking, you will become far more successful. When you get up in front of an entire room of individuals and tell them you are a real estate investor and that you're looking to partner with some private lenders, you will be very surprised how many people are interested.

3. **We stay inside our normal circles.** This is one area where I will tell you to get away from your normal real estate investor club. You may meet some private lenders there, but competition from other investors will naturally drive up the price. You need to get into some other networking groups or local organizations where you can meet people who are not involved in real estate. They will be attracted to you since you are a real estate expert. In their eyes, you know a whole lot more than they do since they know nothing. Your goal is to build rapport and then ask them to partner with you.

4. **We don't portray ourselves as an expert.** You need to get good at analyzing deals and learning how to talk about investment returns in public. We often teach our mentoring students how to run quick numbers in their head to simply

analyze an investment. This will really help you look like an expert when you are talking to potential lenders. Learn how to talk about the deals you are working on and watch their trust grow and the dollar signs shine in their eyes.

5. **We don't talk about our successes.** Once you get a deal under your belt, one where you worked with a private money partner, you need to tell everyone you meet about it. Your private lender may not want to be mentioned by name, but that doesn't mean you can't talk about the deal itself. Just tell them all about the deal. Maybe your total amount invested, including purchase price, repairs, and soft costs, was $150K. You brought in a private money partner and gave him a 12% net return on his money, and guaranteed him $10K if he put the money up. You sold the deal for $250K and earned a nice spread. Your private lender was happy and he wants to do another deal. Now, your marketing and reputation just got very powerful. You have a story to tell, and as long as you keep telling it to people, the money will continue to roll in. It's all about getting the first deal under your belt and then telling others about it.

When we first launched our turn-key real estate investor business, we got really good at marketing to find motivated sellers. We ended up with more deals in our pipeline than we had buyers to sell them to. We needed to unload some inventory, so we began telling every-one we knew about the deals. Eventually, we were approached by an investor with cash who asked if we needed to borrow any private money. He didn't make us order an appraisal; all he cared about was the fact that he liked the deal. We ended up borrowing the funds from him for 90 days as transactional money. We guaranteed him a

$1,000 minimum for putting up the funds. We have now done over 50 deals with this particular individual, and we have a long list of lenders waiting for a deal. We ended up developing this system to find private money and do more deals by accident, and you can do it too. Focus on the deal, get the word out, and the money will come.

So, as you can see, there is more money out there in consumers' bank accounts than there are deals. Finding private money is not your problem. Talking to consumers about your deals and selling them on why they should work with you is your problem. Learn how to master these tactics and there will be no limit to the number of profitable deals you can do!

SECTION III

Sharpen Your Technical Toolbox

CHAPTER 13

Business Planning

You don't need a business plan to buy, sell, and rent a couple of houses. If, however, you desire to build a real estate business—or a portfolio that will provide earned income for you and your family, a retirement income, and an inheritance for your heirs—then a good business plan is an absolute necessity. I am not talking about a plan with hundreds of pages, filled with intricate details. I am talking about a simple outline that should be developed for your own use. My business plan is only a dozen pages in length, and I review and update it every January. This review helps me to focus and make the adjustments necessary to operate in the current and anticipated future market.

With that in mind, let's take a look at how you can create a simple business plan.

Creating a Simple Business Plan

I've found that there are 8 steps to creating a basic business plan.

Step 1—Settle on the basics first. Before beginning your business plan, you may want to review Part I of this book. Until you are absolutely settled on where you are, where you want to be, and your time frame for getting there, you are not ready to do any planning. Once you are sure of these facts, write a brief synopsis of them at the top of your business plan.

Step 2—Focus on your destination. Once you've figured out what you want to achieve, establish the weekly activity necessary to meet your goals. Let's look at an example of this process. Please note that this example is simplified and not necessarily indicative of real-world numbers. I just want you to learn the process. Let's begin by assuming your goal is to buy 12 houses in a given year, and you have decided to buy these houses by sending letters directly to absentee landlords. Perhaps you have discussed this with other more experienced investors, and they have given you the following advice. You need to mail 100 letters to get five responses, and you can expect to buy a house after speaking with 20 probable sellers. Since your goal is to buy 12 houses per year, you need to make one purchase each month. Now, to buy a single house, you'll need to deal with 20 absentee owners, and to get 20 owners to call you, you'll need to mail out 400 letters a month—or approximately 100 letters each week.

What you have just done is convert a goal into actionable weekly activity. If a week passes and you have not mailed 100 new letters, you have not done the necessary work to accomplish your goal. Whether your task is buying houses, selling houses, building a rental portfolio, obtaining private financing, or any other task, breaking it down into actionable pieces will allow you to accurately track your progress. Good sales trainers teach their students that if they need to ask 100 people to buy their product to close a sale, and the first 10 say no, they should smile and be happy since they are already 10% along the path to a successful sale. Remember how an ant eats an elephant: one bite at a time.

Step 3—Identify the tools you will need to accomplish your goals. Here are a few tools that have helped Adam and I along the way:

- **Real Estate Associations.** Networking at local real estate social groups—and becoming involved with real estate educational groups—will provide you with a forum to expand your knowledge, talk with like-minded individuals, and obtain referrals for other people and businesses you will need on your team.

- **Education/Mentoring.** This may be someone who will allow you to apprentice with them, or simply a favorite educator who teaches specifically within the field of your chosen path. I chose to glean all that I could from books, and from speakers at various events, and I have never worked for anyone else in this business. Most of my basic real estate education was obtained pre-internet, but in today's world, a simple search will reveal massive resources for education. Do not, however, buy any education until you finish this book. I have seen new investors waste tens of thousands of dollars on education that did not move them any closer to their goals.
- **Key Professionals and Tradesmen.** A good title company that is experienced working with investors is a must. A real estate attorney, insurance agent, contractor, subcontractors, and suppliers are among the professionals that you may need on your team.

Step 4—Identify your markets. You need to determine and describe the specific market that you'll be operating in. Adam and I chose to provide turn-key rental property to true hands-off investors. More specifically, our houses are sold cash-only. So our buyers are either retirees or professionals who are still working. In either case, they must have cash reserves adequate to buy one or more houses. These buyers expect an average spendable return of 9-12%. Since our houses must return a profit for us, while still providing acceptable returns to our buyers, we have found that 2- or 3-bedroom houses in working-class neighborhoods are the best vehicle. These houses are available in certain neighborhoods in North and West Jacksonville.

You might want to further break down your market to include other resources, such as renovation assets, marketing resources, and so on.

Step 5—Build your methodology. Here you need to get specific about *how* you will accomplish your goals. You should categorize methodology by function. For example, if the function is buying, you need to describe the exact houses and neighborhoods where you want to buy, and describe how you will market to find motivated sellers. Do the same with every function necessary for your success.

Step 6—Create a financial overview. You need to state basics of where the money you need will come from, how much money you will need, and repayment terms that fit with your plans.

Step 7—Identify key issues. This is a pretty dynamic field as your key issues will tend to change as your business evolves and with changing market conditions. Just try to identify the critical issues you can see right now. An example of a critical issue might be learning how to write a good buyer's letter.

Step 8—Create a guide for motivation and focus. Here you should list what motivated you, including key phrases and/or quotes that you have found valuable. One word of caution: *Your business plan is a tool and not a secret weapon that will propel you to success.* By writing down your plan, you will create a roadmap in your mind that will help you to remain focused on your goals and the action required to meet those goals. Never be afraid to revise your plan. Markets change constantly resulting in a need for methodology adjustments. You will also learn and grow in confidence, and as you do, you will want to take full advantage of your increased knowledge to apply your assets and resources more efficiently.

Joe's Sample Business Plan

Now that we've covered the basics, I want to share one of my early business plans with you. I don't share my current business plan as it contains a lot of personal information. Concentrate on the form and not the actual names and specific resources listed. Please also note that the process described above does not exactly match the business plan I've shared below. The following plan is from many years ago, and I have refined the process over the years.

Ten-Year Goals
1. Maintain an annual income of $130K.
2. Build cash flow at the rate of $3K/year.
3. Build an estate of $2M in NET performing assets (equities) within six years.
4. Convert $2M in equities to "auto-pilot" at an 11% net return by August of 2012.

My Team
1. Joe Locklear, Principal
2. Jacksonville Real Estate Investors Marketplace
3. Individuals & IRAs, Rehab Financier
4. Navigator Mortgage, Refinance Broker
5. Laura Riebsame, All Florida Title Co.
6. Diane at A&B Insurance
7. Adam Locklear, Locklear Real Estate Partners
8. Jax Family Housing, Inc., Holding Co.
9. Community Building & Restoration, Inc.
10. Equity Trust, Inc., Self-Directed IRA Custodian

Market Summary
1. Buy rental houses based on cash flow only.

2. Buy rental property ONLY in areas with favorable ratios (North and West Jacksonville).
3. All portfolio properties must be newly professionally renovated with low maintenance components.
4. New construction on infill lots only, no land development.

Methodology
1. Income generated by sale of new construction and renovated rental property.
2. Cash flow generated by owning rental properties.
3. Performing assets developed by buying below market value, reducing debt, and directly managing renovations.
4. Roth IRA used to shelter all income over $100K per year.
5. Acquisition via proprietary marketing program, with direct purchasing by Joe Locklear and MLS purchasing by Adam Locklear.
6. Top professional management for construction operations by Adam Locklear of Locklear Realty.
7. Portfolio property professionally managed by Adam Locklear of Locklear Realty.

Financial Overview
1. Construction funded by individual lenders through equity lines, savings (IRAs), and institutional lenders.
2. Rehabbed properties are refinanced for increased cash flow through Navigator Mortgage (refinance broker).
3. Cash flow funded by rental receipts.

Key Issues—Near Term
1. Solidify construction management operations/increase production through standardization.

2. Reduce interim funding costs of new construction and rehabs (ongoing) by expanding private sources and decreasing the need for institutional financing.

3. Reduce long-term interest costs and increase availability of private long-term mortgages (ongoing).

4. Refine the automation process for purchasing land and distressed houses.

Key Issues—Long Term

1. Replace all earned income with passive income.

2. Train my replacement.

Focus and Perseverance

Nothing worthwhile was intended to be fast or easy. No one becomes great overnight, but you can become great over time. The longest distance between two points is called a "shortcut." Stop looking for magic beans and quick fixes and devote yourself to the disciplines necessary to steadily accelerate your growth. Identify critical issues required to move your business forward, then manage those issues daily—every day without fail. Don't make things more difficult by failing to focus. All you need to do is learn to execute ordinary things extraordinarily well. Adjust technique, but never take your eyes off your goals. Success depends less on the brilliancy of your plan and more on the consistency of your actions.

From this sample plan, I hope you can see how simple an effective business plan can be. Remember that you are writing this plan for your own use. Keep it simple and keep it up to date.

Adam's Take on Business Planning

Having an effective business plan is a cornerstone for success in business. It's not enough to just have a plan in your head or an idea of what you want to do. When I graduated college, the first thing I did in real estate was manage rental properties. I did a good job collecting rent and marketing the properties to find quality tenants who wanted to live in affordable rental units. Word soon got around about my skills, and I was able to quickly build a thriving property management business.

I went from managing a few rental properties that my family owned to managing over 200 houses for investors in a relatively short period of time. I was making a good living for a young guy just out of college, but I soon ran into a myriad of growth headaches. The problem was I hadn't planned for the growth. I had no idea of who to hire, how much to pay them, or what they would be doing. Have you ever owned a business? Do you know someone who has? Does this sound at all familiar to you? So, I hired a few employees to handle some tasks and help bring in new clients and retain quality tenants, but I soon ran into another problem. A few months after hiring my new employees, I ran out of cash.

I wasn't able to cover my office rent, and I was barely making payroll. Vendors were asking to be paid, and one of my property owners didn't get his rental check that month. Undercapitalization is the major reason why most businesses do not make it through the first few years. Needless to say, I had no money after all the expenses were paid, and I was flat broke. I ended up letting a vendor go, and I was forced to bring in a working partner who had some cash saved up just to make it through that quarter.

Now if I had sat down with a consultant from day one and mapped out a formal business plan, I would have been way better off in the long run. The happy part of this story is I was eventually able to get some help, and I did put together a formal business plan a few years later. My business consultant helped me get my books in order, focus on key hiring, and turn my productivity into profit.

We actually ended up scaling the business back instead of growing. We fixed the problems we had and nailed down our bottom line. After that, we began to grow again, and this time it was healthy growth. We had an awesome business plan to follow, and I was blessed enough to eventually sell Locklear Property Management for a big chunk of cash. Selling my first business was a rush, and I owe it all to my business consultant who helped me develop a formal business plan to maximize my profit and encouraged healthy growth.

If you want to be successful as a real estate investor, it is paramount that you commit your business plan to paper. Once you get it on paper, start sharing it with some influential people who are good at business. You can find local business networks through an organization known as Business Networking International (BNI). They have chapters in almost every city, and you can meet some sharp business people there—many of whom would be willing to help you just to see you succeed. You need to seek out mentors who will help you develop your business plan. The Small Business Administration (SBA) also has some great resources for helping new and existing small business owners develop a formal plan. Once you get the skeleton of your plan together, you can apply it to your chosen real estate investment path.

Please spend some quality time developing your plan, and remember: The best plans are those that are built to adapt to market changes. I wish you the greatest success with your real estate investing business plan, and if you need any help putting it together, please let us know.

CHAPTER 14

Asset Protection

Real estate asset protection is not a standardized subject. There are no "one size fits all" solutions. Effective asset protection must be tailored to all aspects of a deal. If you do the same types of deals over and over as we do, it will be easier to develop an asset protection strategy. If the types of deals you work on vary, and if you operate different business entities or work with different partners each time, you will need professional assistance. I want to make sure you understand that I am not qualified to give you legal advice. I am simply telling you how I protect my assets. You should consult your attorney before implementing any asset protection strategy.

The majority of our business is conducted within our turn-key real estate investment company. We locate and buy distressed properties, renovate those properties, and resell them to other long-term investors. We also purchase houses that we hold as rentals in our own personal portfolios. I am going to tell you how we approach asset protection for our particular operations. Again, this is a subject with many different opinions. Please also note that we are in Florida. If your business is located in a different state, your laws will be different. Below is an outline of the asset protection plan that we have developed for our Florida operations.

Insurance Protection

Asset protection begins with adequate insurance. Never close any house purchase until an insurance binder is in place. A binder is a document provided by an insurance company to the closing parties stating that insurance is in place and describing the basic details of coverage. This binder comes from your insurance company, based on your request. It is accompanied by an invoice. Once the title agent cuts a check to the insurance company, the policy is bound and in full effect.

Although we occasionally buy a tenant-occupied policy, 95% of our purchases are vacant, distressed homes in need of renovations. We purchase two types of property insurance for these: liability and comprehensive. The liability protects us from potential lawsuits if someone is injured on the property (unless they are working on the property), and comprehensive protects the property from perils like storm and fire damage. Policies vary greatly between different providers, so to steal a line from Ronald Reagan, "Trust but verify." It is important to build a relationship of trust with your insurance agent, but you must also read your policy. Do not assume any coverage that is not specifically expressed in your policy.

If we buy an occupied property, we can purchase a landlord policy that is similar to a homeowner's policy. This policy costs us around $50-$60 monthly, and if we cancel, any unearned premium is refundable. Insurance for an unoccupied property in need of repairs is a different type of policy. We call this type of policy a "vacant policy," and it is similar to builder's risk insurance commonly purchased when building a new home. Vacant policies cost us about $200 monthly and there are no refunds. We typically purchase a 60- or 90-day policy at closing in order to give us time to do the repairs. Once repairs are done, we convert over to the less expensive landlord policy.

Some investors will understate the need for repairs, represent that the property is ready for occupancy, and buy the landlord coverage.

Do not do this as the insurance company will likely deny any claim occurring before occupancy. This is not an area to save a few bucks. Good insurance is your first line of defense against loss of your investment and possible loss of additional assets.

In the state of Florida, the type of liability described above will not protect you from a lawsuit by anyone working on your property. You are responsible for making sure that everyone working on your property is covered with worker's compensation insurance, or possesses a valid, state-issued exemption. In order to apply for an exemption from worker's compensation insurance, a worker must be a business entity (corporation or LLC). You must pay the exemption holder (business entity) directly, and the exemption holder must have a copy of his or her exemption on their person when on any jobsite. The business entity may exempt more than one person, but every exempted person must hold a certain percentage of ownership in the business entity. I know that this sounds onerous and unfair to a property owner, but it is the law in Florida.

We do allow workers with exemptions on our projects in all trades except roofing and electrical. Roofing and electrical work are inherently dangerous. An exempted worker is responsible for their own hospital bills, and even a life insurance policy may hesitate to pay a claim when worker's compensation is exempted. Remember, if you choose to act as your own contractor, then you are a contractor, and you had better learn the rules! Have you seen all the ads from hungry attorneys looking for an easy mark? Get good insurance and save yourself the headaches.

Business Entity

Second to having good insurance is your choice of a business entity. My attorney prefers corporations to LLCs, so we are incorporated. He tells me that there is a hundred years of case law on corporations and only a few on LLCs. I guess he is somewhat "old school," but so am I. My son Adam often calls me a dinosaur, but of course never hesitates to ask for my antiquated opinion. A lot of investors prefer LLCs, so it would seem they are also a valid entity for asset protection.

Land Trusts

Last (but not least) is the use of a land trust. Years ago, you only had land trusts in Illinois and Florida. Today, most states have provisions for the use of land trusts to own real estate. I know about Florida land trusts, so that is the only type of land trust I am going to discuss. A Florida land trust is an entity created to own real property in the state of Florida. The trust consists of a written and signed agreement, a trustee, and a beneficiary (and possibly contingent beneficiaries). The land trust owns the property and the beneficiary owns the land trust. The trustee simply signs documents and is, in effect, simply a secretary. Sounds like a corporation, right? Well, it is somewhat similar in function with three major differences. It is these differences that make it an invaluable tool for asset protection:

1. Land trusts do not have to be recorded to be valid, so short of a court order, there is no way for a person outside the trust to identify the true owner of the trust (beneficiary).
2. Land trusts may be transferred with a simple assignment document.
3. As long as you have a good and valid land trust form, there is no cost to establish the trust.

Here are a couple of situations where land trusts are useful…

1. **Your tenant gets a leak from the air conditioner, slips on the water, and sues you for a back injury.** The first thing

any attorney will do is check on the assets of the probable defendant. They do a name search and see that you only own your homestead. Not even the rental property where the tenant fell is under your name. Next, they look up the tenant's address and see that it is in a land trust. They determine that your homestead is exempt from any lawsuit if it is not actually involved in the accident and that the rental property is only worth $50,000. Their decision might be to proceed with a settlement with your insurance company as the insurance limit is greater than your obtainable assets.

I'll bet that if you had owned 20 houses in your personal name, they would have been salivating at the chance of going after you. You may not own 20 houses, but you might own 20 land trusts that own one house each. Remember, land trusts are not recorded. The deed held by the trust is recorded, but the deed does not contain the name of the beneficiary (owner) of the trust. Land trusts are only responsible for the assets listed within that specific trust document. Most attorneys prefer an easy mark and have no desire to enter a lengthy battle to penetrate multiple land trusts. This situation is precisely why you should never tell anyone how many houses you own.

2. **You want to flip a property that you are buying from a bank, but the contract states that you cannot assign to a new buyer.** That's a simple one. Just make your offer in the name of a land trust and assign the land trust to your secondary buyer. This is 100% legal and practical as you did not assign a new buyer for the property. You simply made an offer to sell the land trust that owns it. The trust never sold or released the actual property, and there are no restrictions on selling land trusts. If there is a period re-

quired before you can resell, just wait until the ownership can transfer to any entity the buyer desires. I have done this literally hundreds of times. If you go this route, it is important to work with a closing attorney or title company that is familiar with land trusts.

It is important you understand that land trusts are not foolproof. If a court order is obtained, a judge can force you to proclaim all your assets. But, in theory, an attorney would have no reason to go there unless they suspected you owned unregistered assets. A land trust is only responsible for those assets listed within that specific trust.

Here is a summary of how we approach asset protection:

1. We make all offers to purchase in the name of a land trust.
2. If we want to sell our interest before closing, we do an agreement with our buyer to assign the land trust to them at closing. They agree to allow their purchase money to fund the closing. Some IRA custodians will not allow the beneficiary to fund a simultaneous closing. In that case, we (or one of our private investors) fund the first closing.
3. We always have an adequate insurance binder sent to, paid for, and issued at closing.
4. We only use workers who have either a worker's compensation policy (or exemption), and we do not accept exemptions for the more dangerous trades like roofing or electrical.

Many investors add another layer of protection. They form a business entity and buy the property in a trust with the entity (usually an LLC) as the beneficiary. Adam and I do not do this as we feel that LLCs, being subject to state regulations, must be registered with an agent and must be reported and renewed periodically. LLCs are also costly if you want them to keep your assets separate. To do this, you would need to form, register, and maintain a separate LLC for each property. Some investors will place several properties in a single LLC. However, we feel this strategy defeats the purpose as a suit against any property in the LLC could tie them all up.

Land trusts are free and unregistered, so we use them religiously. We feel that good insurance is our first and best line of defense. Consider the highest available liability limits on your policy, plus buying an umbrella policy. If you want more protection, have an LLC or corporation own the trust. The ultimate protection, in our opinion, would be to own each property in a land trust with its own separate LLC or corporation as the beneficiary. A good insurance agent who is used to working with real estate investors is an absolute must.

Adam's Take on Protecting Your Assets

When you start building up your net worth and rental property portfolio, you will become a target. I am not claiming to be a rock star or anything here, but I have experienced what success feels like. My wife, Patricia, and I have been blessed enough to upgrade our primary home to a nice neighborhood that has its own yacht club. I won't go into too much detail, but we are comfortable with our current business and living situation. Once we began to enter a higher income bracket, the wolves began knocking on our door. I am not even kidding.

The day after we moved into our new home, a salesman started beating on our front door exclaiming, "Welcome to the neighborhood! How would you like to buy some energy-efficient, high-grade windows?" I was literally holding a moving box, with sweat pouring down from moving couches around. We started getting tons of credit card offers in the mail, our bank was always asking us to refinance our home, and we immediately started getting luxury magazines to buy cars and join local country clubs.

The short story is this: Everyone out there wants your money! If you are not smart with it, and if you fail to set up some lines of defense, you are going to get picked off by the pack and chewed up for breakfast. You need to learn how to protect your assets, my friend. Joe has already given you some solid tactics and tools you can use to protect yourself in conducting transactions. That being said, I am going to tell you it won't be enough. The problem is, the wolves are rabid and they exist all over the world. Once you move into the better neighborhood or operate a thriving business, there is going to be public information out there that you will be unable to control.

Follow This Foolproof Method to Protect Your Assets

I am not an attorney, and I would never give you legal advice. The best part about that line is it's so much fun for me to say! You see, I was pre-law in my undergraduate college studies among other things. The truth is, I was a good student growing up, but by the time I reached high school, I had lost all my motivation and graduated as a C student. When I began taking law classes, they were hard for me. I was behind on my studies and I had to work hard to catch up. I put countless hours into reading my law textbooks, and I often visited my law professors' offices for advice and tutoring, and to pick their brains. One day I strolled into my professor's office and asked, "What is the best way to protect your assets?" The answer came back: "It depends." This is one of the best lessons I learned in pre-law.

My professor was of the opinion that each and every person in the world has a different level of happiness, net worth, and experience. We can group people into different income classes and social groups, but at the core of who we are is an individual with specific needs, desires, and resources. These different variables lead us to a custom approach for developing a plan to protect our assets. Joe and I can tell you how to get around banks not allowing you to assign a contract by using a land trust, and we can tell you how to reduce your risk by buying liability insurance. But we can't tell you *exactly* how to structure your business or personal assets. So, how does the foolproof method work if we can't tell you what to do? The answer is simple: You need to build an asset protection team.

Who to Add to Your Asset Protection Team

When you're organizing and building your team, I want you to follow one simple rule. This one simple rule is going to be the best piece of advice you get on this subject. I can say that because this simple rule was passed on to me by a very smart and successful businessman in Florida. So, here is the rule. I want you to write this down and staple it on your office wall or any place where you'll see it regularly. Are you ready? Ok, here we go: **Only hire the best**.

That's it! You need to stop being cheap and go out and discover the best professionals in your area who can help you structure your business and life to protect your assets. Once I stopped being cheap and started following this mentality, I was able to structure my life for success. I haven't looked back since and things just keep getting better.

Here's what my dream team looks like:

1. **Business Attorney.** A business attorney is useful for guiding you into setting up your business entity. Whether you decide to go with an LLC, an S-Corp, or a C-Corp, your business attorney will help you get set up. They will register with your state and help you structure your business entity documents. This type of attorney is also very good at writing corporate documents and contracts, and can even

write basic leases, joint venture agreements, confidentiality agreements, and more. Do not be cheap. Get the best business attorney in town! He will pay for his services by protecting you with iron-clad agreements and a proper business structure.

2. **Real Estate Attorney.** This type of attorney is an expert in real estate agreements and transactions. Your real estate attorney can do everything from writing complicated residential and commercial leases to handling your actual title searches and real estate closings. Once again, get the best real estate attorney in town. We had our real estate attorney write our land trust agreement, and that one document has helped us earn hundreds of thousands of dollars on wholesaling bank foreclosure deals. We paid him well for writing that document, but it's paid for itself thousands of times over by now.

3. **Financial Planner.** This team member will actually help you in general with your financial plan. My personal financial planner helped me set up my kids' college funds, my IRA account, my wife's financial accounts, our life insurance policies, our disability insurance policies, and a myriad of other products and resources we needed as entrepreneurs. He helps me max out different savings and investment buckets to decrease my tax burdens and increase my overall net worth. He's very keen on asset growth and protection, and having him on my team helps balance me out in general and increases my growth efforts exponentially. Ask yourself this one question: After you earn all that rent money and investment cash from your real estate endeavors, what are you going to do with it? A good financial planner will help you keep some of your cash liquid and

invest it into other areas that will help you increase the assets for your entire family. They will also help you answer "what if" questions. What if I pass away? What if I get hurt and can't work? It's really easy to burn through all your assets by paying expensive medical bills. Don't be naive. Plan for the worst-case scenario now and protect your family's assets for years to come.

4. **Certified Public Accountant (CPA).** This team member is my personal favorite. Maybe it's because during a dark time in my financial life I hired the best CPA in town and he pulled me from the ashes. He saved me from the mean and ugly IRS monster who wanted to take everything I owned. At the end of my first six-figure year, I received a giant bill from the IRS. They said I owed them $50K, and they wanted to place a lien on my house, which they did. My CPA told me I was doing it all wrong. He told me to stop doing my taxes personally, and he went back and amended my business and personal returns for multiple tax years. Because he's a licensed and highly qualified CPA, he acts as a buffer between me and the IRS. He backs me up and gives me the best advice to save money on my taxes and navigate the ever-sticky tax codes that are constantly changing. Before I start any new ventures, I always pick up the phone and schedule a sit down with my CPA, who analyzes my current situation and gives me the best tax advice. If you fail to hire a highly qualified CPA, it's going to cost you thousands upon thousands of dollars. Do not hire a bookkeeper to do your tax returns. A basic accountant is fine for entering income and expenses into QuickBooks, but they are rarely qualified to provide a high level of asset protection like a good CPA can.

5. **Business Insurance Agent.** This team member can provide you with all of your business insurance protection. They will suggest that you buy errors and omissions insurance to protect your team from contract mistakes and such. They can write policies for your company cars, and even an umbrella policy that can fill in the gaps and protect your business and overall assets where other policies may tap out.

So, there you have it. That's my dream team. These are the professionals I use to protect my personal and business assets. I will remind you once more to get the best team members in the business. Real estate is one of the most complicated industries, and there can be a lot of risks involved if you want to be successful. As you start to grow your net worth, the wolves will appear, so make sure your dream team is in place from the beginning.

CHAPTER 15

Maximizing Profits & Avoiding Gremlins

Just because you purchase a property does not mean that you really own it. In some cases, real estate agents list properties for sale, potential buyers view them and make offers, and then a buyer enters into a contract to purchase with no real assurance that the seller actually owns the property. You may spend a lot of time and effort up front working on a deal only to find out just before closing that there are title problems. The greatest way to kill this demon is to purchase title insurance at closing.

But here's the problem: You may have already spent weeks negotiating and performing due diligence before you sign a contract and order title work. Once ordered, it could take 1-3 weeks to get the report back. Sometimes this cannot be avoided. Until you get the title report, you have no guarantee that your seller has "marketable" title. There are, however, a few things that you can do early in the deal to identify the potential for title problems.

Title and Legal Issues

Past deeds tell a story. A search of the local property appraiser's website should reveal a list of the last five or six deeds recorded for the property. Most appraiser's offices use the same national software to list and record transactions, and searching this database is usually pretty simple. You don't really need to read each deed, just pay attention to what "type" of deed you are viewing.

General warranty deeds are the most reliable as title insurance was almost certainly issued when the warranty deed was executed. *Special warranty deeds* usually mean the property was foreclosed by the lender, and they are now reselling the property. A foreclosure, if done correctly, eliminated most title problems. Early in our negotiating process, we look up the address at the property appraiser's website. If we see a general or special warranty deed as the last transaction, we will proceed with the negotiating/buying process. If we see that *a tax deed* was recorded less than four years ago, then we know we may have a problem. In the case of a tax deed, we contact the seller and ask if a *suit to quiet title* has been completed.

In the state of Florida, there is a four-year statute of limitations on setting aside tax deeds. This means that if a person can prove they were not properly served, and that they had an interest in the property sold for taxes, then they can sue for their interest. On tax deeds, one of two things must exist in order to get title insurance (assuming everything else is in order). You must either successfully complete a suit for quiet title or wait 48 months from the date of issuance of the tax deed. Quiet title suits can cost between $4,000-$7,000 and can take four months to a year to complete. Make sure to ask your attorney if a quiet title suit will cause the title to be both marketable and insurable. Not every property title can be cured this way, however. If you decide to buy a tax deed property, make sure you allow for the time and expense of curing the title situation. We will buy a tax deed property to place in our private portfolios, but not to resell, and we always get big discounts.

Structural Issues

Structural gremlins can literally make your investment worthless! The first thing I do when inspecting a potential house to buy is to step inside the front door and heavily plod/bounce in a circular motion. I do this in every room. At 200+ pounds, I will detect any floor issues. I can tell from sound and feel if the floors have problems. I know what type of wall cracks matter and which do not. Having both built and renovated hundreds of houses, I know what I am looking for. If you do not possess this level of expertise, and you suspect any structural issues, get help!

Adam and I own a Meetup group with (at the time of this writing) almost 2,000 members. Among these members are a lot of wholesalers. We do buy from wholesalers, but we never depend on a wholesaler to accurately describe a property. Here's how one I looked at recently was described: "Great rental property, just needs a little repair work. Asking $25,000 OBO." When I looked at this particular property, I immediately knew that it had serious slab/footer settlement problems. The front wall was leaning in four inches. Proper structural repairs would cost 5-10 times the property's after-repair value. This was a very bad structure. If it was offered to me for free, with a $5,000 bonus, I would have refused.

I called the wholesaler a week later to see if I could get in to take some pics. I wanted to use them in my "gremlins" class. He told me that the house had been sold. Unfortunately, somebody will lose every penny they invested in this house.

Here are a few structural gremlins to look out for:

Tilted Floors. This is when the floors seem fairly solid, but are not level. In the case where a porch has been enclosed, slanting floors may be normal as they were designed for water to run off. This is, however, undesirable, and you should consider leveling the slanted areas. Another cause of slanted wood-frame floors is settlement of the footings at different rates. Sometimes a wider area of the footing provides firmer support than another narrower section, resulting in uneven settlement. However, there could also be runoff from rainfall undermining the foundations. Tilted floors can be very expensive to fix, and if resulting from inadequate bearing soils, not practical to repair.

Spongy Floors. If floors do not react to bouncing on them and seem "spongy," this is an issue. It may be that the floor joist or perimeter band joist have suffered damage from rot and/or insects. The subfloor may also be particle board and deteriorated.

Cracked Slabs. If you see a crack in a concrete slab that is smaller than a pencil lead, and the crack is level across, it is probably just caused by normal expansion/contraction and not an issue. If, however, the crack is wider than a pencil lead and/or is uneven across, it could be a major problem.

Sagging Beams. Sagging beams are the result of rot/insect damage, inadequate design, or alterations that have increased or moved the load on the beam. It is very common to have a sagging beam between two rooms where a wall was improperly removed. Sagging beams can be repaired, but the repair might require a new post and new concrete footings.

Sagging Roof Trusses. These can be very expensive to repair and will almost always require plans designed by a certified engineer. The entire roof system may have to be removed and replaced. Unless you are an experienced contractor, walk away from houses with sagging roofs.

Tilted or Sagging Walls. This is an indication of serious structural deterioration. If the walls are tilted or sagging excessively, just drive on by.

Missing Footers. In situations where open carports were converted to living areas (very common in Florida) and the work was not permitted, chances are that no footers were installed. When you see a carport-living area conversion, look closely for any structural cracking. You can also check to see if building permits were obtained.

Termite Infestation. We deal with two species of termites here in Florida. The first are subterranean termites. These termites nest in the soil. They build mud tunnels from the ground up to the house. The tunnels look like brown veins or the bare limbs of a skinny bush. They can be treated at the areas of infestation, and the cost of treatment is usually $300-$500. This cost does not include repairing any structural damage caused. If there are drywood termites living in the house, tenting and fumigation will be required. Expect to spend $1,500-$3,000. Drywood termites do not have to go to the ground for moisture. They always swarm toward light, and you should check the window sills for their carcasses. They love to eat wood trim inside the house and will hollow out the trim, leaving most of the paint in place. I have seen houses for sale that were destroyed beyond repair by termites. I have an exterior picture of a nice, straight stucco house that I inspected. When I got inside, the exterior walls were almost nonexistent. Termites had eaten so much that the stucco itself was holding up the roof. If you see any evidence of termites, get a professional inspection.

Low-Slope Shingle Roofs. Fiberglass shingles are by far the most popular residential roofing material used in Florida. Unfortunately, not all roofs have been installed by professionals and misuse of shingles is common. Shingles overlap each other and require a certain minimum slope to function. If they are installed on slopes lower than 2.5 in 12 (a 2.5 foot drop over 12 lineal feet), they will leak and/or blow off in a storm. Slopes lower than 2.5 in 12 require low-slope roofing materials. Modified torch-down is commonly used on low-slope roofs. Modified comes in continuous rolls approximately 36' wide. You can buy an inexpensive slope meter and place it on the roof. If in doubt, get a roof inspection.

Asbestos Siding and Roof Shingles. The only way to verify the presence of asbestos in building materials is to remove a sample and have it lab tested. You can, however, look for signs that would indicate whether asbestos "may" be present. Some fibrous cement wall shingles contained asbestos. If you see thick and/or diamond-shaped roof shingles, they could also contain asbestos. Asbestos is not dangerous unless you inhale the fibers. If the asbestos-containing materials are not ragged, bare, and exposed, they are not a danger, but they should be encapsulated (painted with a thick paint). If you have to re-roof a house with asbestos shingles, you could spend double the amount of a regular roofing job.

Windows. Minimum property standards require windows to have screens and to remain stationary when opened. If they slide shut on their own, they will need repair or replacement. You will need to hire a licensed contractor to replace windows. You can easily spend $3,000 replacing windows on a rental house.

Plumbing. Most homes that we view and make offers on are vacant and the utilities are turned off. This makes plumbing harder to inspect, however, you can get a pretty good idea by looking at the valves and drains under the sinks. If you see galvanized pipe extending through the walls, you will need to repipe as it will almost certainly not provide adequate water pressure. Look for any signs of digging in the yard where the sewer line exits. If you see a gray colored pipe (polybutylene), look at the fittings. If the fittings are plastic, you will have leakage, but if fittings are copper with copper banding, you should be ok. If a well or septic system are present, you will need a professional inspection.

Electrical. Look inside the electrical distribution panel. If it is labeled "Federal Pacific Stab-Loc," it will have to be replaced as these panels are now uninsurable and a fire hazard. There are other local requirements that you may need to familiarize yourself with as well. In Jacksonville, if the power has been off for one year or more, an electrical safety inspection is required before utility service can be turned back on. Since safety codes have changed over the years, you may be forced to upgrade equipment and wiring at substantial cost.

Air Conditioning. The type of Freon used in air conditioning systems has changed over the last few years. The EPA has forced price increases on the old Freon type to a level that makes it very expensive to maintain the older units. Do not assume that an older unit can be repaired cheaply. New equipment could cost you $2,500-$3,500.

Code Enforcement. This gremlin is a sneaky one. You should always check the local municipality for any code enforcement issues. Just because the property is in good condition does not guarantee that there are not past unresolved issues.

Permitting. This gremlin can be a nasty little bugger! It is very common to see homes where a porch or carport has been converted to interior space. If a house you are buying to resell has improvements that were not permitted, the property appraiser may not list the improvements. If your buyer hires an appraiser, the appraiser will almost certainly note unpermitted improvements. This will prevent your buyer from obtaining a loan. There may also be open permits or permits that were pulled, but no final inspection was done. These situations could not only require hiring a contractor to pull new permits and obtain inspections, but the building department could require all improvements to meet current codes, not just the codes that were in place at the time of the improvements. Ouch!

Non-Conventional Construction. We only buy "conventional" houses. Our houses are typical common types that most everyone is comfortable living in. If there are unconventional aspects of a house, it is more difficult to sell or rent. Unconventional issues include round houses, A-frames, low ceilings, narrow and/or steep stairways, bedrooms with no access from a common area, tiny windows, extreme sloping sites, exceptionally small rooms, etc. If you buy an unconventional house, make sure you like it as you may be the only one willing to live in it.

Site Issues. These are issues that exist either due to poor planning or poor construction relating to the physical features of the land. Most site issues are either difficult to correct or not correctable at all. Here are a few site problems commonly encountered:

- **Minimum Setback.** This is usually not an issue unless there is an unpermitted house addition. If a building looks unusually close to a property line, a trip to the municipality is in order. Ask for the minimum setback requirements for the particular house you are considering buying. If you suspect the minimum has been crossed, get a survey.
- **Well-Septic Separation.** If there is both a well and a septic system present on the property, there will be minimum separation requirements. These requirements may not only apply to wells and septic systems on your lot, but also to adjacent lots.
- **Encroachments.** Be careful when you notice an adjacent structure too close to the property lines or crossing it. The laws are different in every state, but most states allow for some form of adverse possession. In extreme cases, ignoring an encroachment issue could cause you to lose title to the land under the encroachment.
- **Drainage Problems.** Site drainage can be a real issue, especially in areas where the land is flat. There are only two places for water on your lot to go—it either runs off or is absorbed by the soil. If the soil is sandy, it will absorb water fairly quickly, but if more clay is present, rainwater will have to either run off or stand until it evaporates. If water has been standing, you can usually see evidence in the form of silt staining in lower areas or on walls. A common problem in Florida is where carports have been closed-in to provide more living area. When most masonry homes were con-

structed with open carports, the carport slabs were poured 4 inches below the main house slabs. On an unpermitted room enclosure, most homeowners built walls right on the existing carport slab. These rooms built on low slabs are very susceptible to water intrusion through the lower walls.

Mold Issues. The mold gremlin is not very sneaky and is very easy to recognize. Mold can be very unruly and scare off a lot of potential buyers. Now this can be a good thing or a bad thing depending on whether you are buying or selling. I was once asked the difference between mold and mildew. My answer was "it's mold when you are buying, and mildew when you are selling." The fact is, all mold can be corrected. The question is the cost. I have bought houses that looked terrible, but all that was necessary to remove the mold was washing and sealing the interior walls. Others I have walked away from as the potential curative cost exceeded the after-repair value of the house. We will often cut out small areas of drywall at different locations to test this. If the backside of all the inspection areas are clean, you should be able to treat the mold from the exterior surface. If you find mold inside the walls, all of the drywall will have to be removed, the interior walls treated, re-insulated, and sealed, and new drywall installed. The cost of this remediation process is usually a deal killer. You will need a professional EPA-certified specialist to clear the dwelling once completed. My advice is to steer clear of serious mold issues.

Special District Compliance. Here in Jacksonville, we deal with three distinct historic districts. You should check with your municipality for the existence of special districts. Requirements for working on houses in special districts are often administered by a specially appointed or elected board of directors. These boards can require special materials and/or construction methods that are not required in other neighborhoods, and these additional requirements can easily double the cost of renovations.

Adam's Take on Maximizing Profits

This chapter is an absolutely amazing cheat sheet! We have spent years in the trenches getting caught by these profit gremlins. I was unusually lucky to have a dad who was out there grinding through tons of transactions, renovations, and real estate deals. Some of the deals he worked on were profitable and some of them not. When Joe talks about the School of Hard Knocks, he is speaking from personal experience. I do have my own hard-earned lessons as well, but more often than not, I learned ahead of time how to avoid making these types of mistakes.

Now, I am not saying that I'm smarter than the average cookie, because, believe me, I'm not. There will always be someone out there who is better looking, smarter, and stronger, or more educated and experienced. The fact is, I had something they did not. I had a real mentor and an honest one who was actually out doing deals, making mistakes, and perfecting his craft. Even though he's my dad, he never handed me anything. But he did educate me on what obstacles existed out there in the real estate investing world. He told me stories about the mistakes he had made, and he encouraged me to not make the same mistakes he had.

I simply cannot overstate or oversell what having a mentor has meant for me in my real estate investing career. It would have taken me a decade longer to get where I am today. So, that's what mentoring was worth to me. Mentoring was worth one decade of my time. The profit gremlins still existed for me, and new ones continue to surface as the real estate market evolves and goes through cycles, but I now have a solid foundation to fall back on when things get tough. I am forever grateful for my real estate investing mentor, and I hope you will find one too.

SECTION IV

Advice From Joe & Adam

CHAPTER 16

Defining Your Success

Where do we find motivation? The phrase "who we are" is often used to describe our "personality," and our personality is greatly influenced by our life experiences. Both positive and negative life events may contribute to our persona and therefore become the seeds of our motivation. The American patriots endured hardships that most of us can only imagine. Many of them sacrificed their fortunes and even their lives, but it was because of their sacrifice and inner "motivation" that our great republic was born. On the other hand, countless successful entrepreneurs enjoyed wealthy parents who nurtured them throughout their childhoods and college years, and helped them to establish their careers.

So, what is success? I like the definition offered by Glenn Bland: "Success is the progressive realization of predetermined, worthwhile goals, stabilized with balance and purified by belief." I have listened to and read books written by most of our era's greatest motivational speakers and authors. I always walk away excited and motivated. External motivation is helpful and uplifting, but it is not sufficient to fuel your path to success. Effective and lasting motivation *always* comes from within.

It took me many years to identify the building blocks of my inner motivation. I recently lost my father, and at his graveside service, we were surprised by the presence of a U.S. Navy Honor Guard. The sharp and crisp sailors spoke of my dad's World War II service in the

South Pacific, neatly folded the American flag that draped his coffin, and placed the flag in my lap. The leader of the Honor Guard then looked directly into my eyes and thanked me for my father's service. At that moment, I recognized the primal source of my motivation.

My father came from humble beginnings. Born in 1925, he grew up in the midst of the Great Depression. He once joked that they knew the depression was over when "a gopher turtle made it all the way across the road." His father died when he was only a year old. He was abandoned by his mother and raised by his two aunts. Although he never completed the sixth grade, he worked hard to earn his GED, and worked even harder to become an educated and experienced tradesman. He was one of only a few men in the city to hold advanced certifications in sheet metal mechanics, ship fitting, and welding. He mainly worked in the sheet metal union, but when work was scarce, his ship fitting and welding skills allowed him to work at the shipyards.

One of my earliest memories was riding with my mom to drop off my dad at the local gas station. There was no other work, so he took a job pumping gas for 50 cents an hour. My dad's pride was always secondary to his love of and dedication to his family. To this day, I can still hear my father telling me that I was special and smart and could become anything that I wanted to be. I would be satisfied to achieve even half of my dad's success. The greatest evidence of success is not the size of our bank account but the legacy that we leave behind on this earth.

Perhaps you're thinking, "It was easy for you. Your dad was a positive role model. I wasn't so lucky." Well, let me tell you the story of my close friend Tom.

Like me, Tom was born in Jacksonville, Florida. His parents split up when he was very young, and his dad died before he really knew him. Although Tom's mother was busy making a living, she was dedicated to her only son. After Tom finished high school, he went to work in a paper mill. Years later, the mill closed. During this time, Tom had a next door neighbor named Bill. Bill was an auto mechanic, but he had been recently exposed to a real estate "guru." Since the mill had closed and Tom was out of work, Bill convinced him to get involved in real estate investing. Now Tom knew absolutely nothing about real estate, but he listened to Bill and others and began to borrow private money, find distressed houses, fix them up, and rent them out. When I met Tom, he was remodeling houses himself, locating tenants, and collecting rent.

We are all different. I was not suited to do exactly what Tom or Bill did. I grew to prefer delegating more to others and concentrating on building a company. Tom introduced me to his neighbor Bill who had developed a wealth of creative real estate techniques. I learned about private financing, land trusts, self-directed IRAs, and many other powerful and effective techniques from Bill.

I still talk with Tom on a daily basis. He continues to be very hands-on, and he's currently working on getting his thirtieth house paid off. Do the math and you will realize that the net passive retirement income from owning 30 free and clear houses is about $15,000 a month. Not bad for a North Jacksonville boy who was raised by a single mother and barely finished high school. Like me, Tom is a graduate of the School of Hard Knocks and a charter member of the Good Old Boys' Club.

I believe that the seeds of success reside within every human being and are the "signature" of our Creator. I hope that you will both discover and learn to nurture the seeds of success residing within you. But before you move further along your path, please take a moment to contemplate your personal definition of "success."

Adam's Take on Success

This is such an important chapter. How do we define our success? You've heard us speak at the end of some of these chapters about what we have done and what we recommend you should be doing to achieve success in real estate investing. There's just one problem with writing a book that tells readers what they need to do if they want to be successful: We have no earthly idea how you define success.

In an effort to explore what some people define as success, I want to go through a few real-life scenarios to get your juices flowing and get you thinking about what you define as your ultimate success. There have been far too many get-rich-quick schemes and motivational books written that define success by how many dollars you can stuff into your checking account. While money does help, it sure won't bring you lasting happiness.

Haitians Are Happier Than You!

Are you familiar with the island nation of Haiti? Haiti is the poorest country in the western hemisphere and is a true third-world country. The gross domestic product per capita (or the average income per resident) was $727.78 per year in 2015. That's only $1.99 per day to live on! This isn't even enough for fresh water. 80% of the population lives below the poverty line, and there is no middle class to speak of in Haiti. Education is not free, and life has been very hard since Haiti was decimated in 2010 by a 7.0 earthquake that turned their capital city of Port Au Prince into rubble. Since then, Haiti has been plagued by starvation, hurricanes, flooding, droughts, disease, drug cartels, government scandals—and pretty much anything else you can think of that would make life miserable.

In 2013, my wife, Patricia, and I had the opportunity to visit Haiti. We were working with our local community church, which had plans to build a school and an orphanage in the poorest area in Haiti. The city of Canaan, where we planned to develop, wasn't a city at all. It was a dumping ground where the good old Haitian government had decided to dump the earthquake victims who had lost their homes and had no money. After the earthquake hit, the FEMA camps filled up, and many people were relocated into the middle of an arid desert with little food and no running water. The residents had to work together and rummage what resources they could find to build their new town and tap into the water supply.

When we hit the ground in Haiti, things were hectic. Their airport is still the worst I have ever seen. The presence of automatic rifles carried by locals was scary. We weren't surprised by the lack of smiles on the residents' faces as we left the airport terminal. What we were surprised by was the love of the people and the sparkling look in their eyes by the time we reached Canaan. I was walking across the street, fresh off the bus to deliver a meal to feed a small village, and a kid tugged on my pant leg. I looked down expecting him to ask for money or food, and all he did was smile at me and hug my leg. Later that day, we held a soccer clinic where residents came out in droves and schooled us with their Haitian soccer skills. They wore giant smiles and they asked for nothing. Women laughed in the streets and entire families who had been displaced from their homes, and were living in the mud, chuckled as they passed the time together. It soon occurred to me that these people laughed more, talked more, and spent more time together, and they loved more passionately, than anyone in my local community.

Yes, it's true. Haitians are more passionate about life than I am. They're probably more passionate about life than you are, too. In spite of everything, Haitians are still happier than we are.

How to Define Your True Success

So, if the poorest of the poor living in one of the worst countries on earth are happier than us, then what have they discovered that we haven't? The simple answer is *time*. Haitians have more time on their hands than you or I do. America is stuck on fast-forward, and if you are reading this in another developed country, then you are likely on fast-forward as well. Our global economy and the rise of technology has shrunk the world we live in and forced us to play catch up.

Haitians have also figured out that the best thing they can do with their time is to spend it with their family, friends, and loved ones. This doesn't mean they are not hard workers. They work all day, but they have figured out how to do it stress-free and how to form strong bonds and lasting relationships. After visiting Haiti and growing my real estate investing companies, I have now discovered my bar for success in life. Yes, I want to build up my net worth, own cash-producing rental homes, grow my businesses, and protect my assets. But what I value more than anything is quality time with my loved ones. When I pass on, I sure as heck won't be able to take a bunch of stuff to the grave with me. When I lay on my death bed, I want to reflect back on all those times laughing with my kids, quality moments spent with my wife, and the precious moments that mold us into who we are.

Still, I can't define your success. You must discover that on your own. I hope these stories and examples will speak volumes to you. I hope you will take some time now and reflect on who you are. Are you writing passionate chapters in the book of your life? Are you who you want to be? Are you defining success in a way that will lead to your ultimate happiness and legacy? If not, you may want to change how you define success. I wish you all the best in life, and I will forever be rooting for your countless future successes!

CHAPTER 17

Our Mistakes Revealed

I always like to begin with the negatives and finish up on a positive note, so let's start this chapter by looking at the various mistakes I have made along my path to real estate success. Over time, I eventually corrected most of these mistakes. As previously stated, I am a graduate of the School of Hard Knocks and the tuition at this university is *very* expensive. By sharing my story, I hope that you can avoid some of the mistakes I have made.

Property Management Mistakes

As I said earlier, landlords tend to be unhappy people. You're much better off hiring a professional property manager to deal with the daily aspects of managing your rentals, but that's not the only mistake you can make. Let's take a look at my top three property management mistakes:

1. Allowing my tenants to know that I owned the property I managed.
2. Allowing my tenants to get my personal cell phone number.
3. Inadequately renovating and maintaining my properties.

All of these mistakes can be summed up to "managing my own properties." After a couple of years, I realized that I was a terrible property manager. There was no consistency with me; I either wanted to kill my tenants or buy and deliver groceries to them. Had I not turned my houses over to a property manager, I would have left the business. I literally hated property management. I also learned that nice, clean houses attract nice, clean renters. Providing better renovated and cleaner homes earned me better, longer-term tenants and actually saved me money.

Property Renovation Mistakes

If you don't know what you're doing, it's easy to lose money when you're doing a renovation. Let's take a look at my top renovating mistakes:

1. Buying cheap, used appliances.
2. Installing cheap, used air conditioning units.
3. Giving advance payments to workers or subcontractors.
4. Physically doing my own renovations and maintenance.

Before entering the real estate investing business, I had a career as a project manager for a large construction company. I knew how to do renovation work and was always tempted to do the physical work myself. However, I soon learned that this was a good way to make $20 or less an hour. It was not useful in moving my real estate career forward. I also learned that appliances, plumbing, and air conditioners create most of your service calls and that investing in new equipment was well worth it. By the time you go back and work on the used stuff, you'll have easily spent enough to have bought new, warrantied appliances and equipment.

Personal Portfolio Building Mistakes

This is another area where I stumbled in the beginning. Here are my top three portfolio building mistakes:

1. Borrowing from banks instead of from individuals.
2. Thinking of my investments as "houses" and not as an "income stream."
3. Spending time trying to buy rental houses in retail neighborhoods.

Hindsight is always 20/20. Looking back, it took me several years to learn that it is better to borrow from individuals. Had I developed and utilized my 984 Loan Program earlier in my career, I would own several more houses than I do.

I would also have avoided trying to make marginal deals in more expensive neighborhoods work as cash-flow rentals. I was never able to buy those houses, and I was like a Bulldog chasing parked cars. I eventually got tired of having my nose flattened and learned to cull out the unworkable deals early in the process.

House Flipping Mistakes

Flipping houses can be a rewarding real estate investing path, but you need to know what you're doing to make it profitable. Here are the top five mistakes I made when I first got started doing retail fix-and-flip deals:

1. Working too hard for too little profit.
2. Not spending enough on renovation to bring properties to the very top of the market.
3. Failing to hire a home stager.
4. Inadequate marketing and not hiring the best real estate agent in town.
5. Speculating on anticipated future market conditions.

If you are going to flip houses, you need to bring the houses up to the top of the market for the neighborhood, and you must be in a neighborhood where houses are selling quickly. Trying to retail properties in a rental or marginal neighborhood is a big mistake. I eventually realized that doing a retail flip involving renovations is a lot more work than renovating a smaller property for rental. I compromised by learning to buy, renovate, and sell rental properties to other "hands-off" investors.

Wealth Building Mistakes

This is another area where I stumbled in the beginning. There are loads of books out there that'll tell you how to get rich quick, but I've found that slow and steady wins the race. When it comes to building wealth, let's take a look at my top five mistakes:

1. Failing to properly utilize my assets and abilities (following the wrong path).
2. Not listening to proven experts. Instead, I relied on "gurus" who wanted to sell me education.
3. Failing to maximize the use of other people's money (OPM) on terms that I established.
4. Letting my pride stand in the way. I had to experience failure to learn I was not "invincible."
5. Being too impatient. I failed to understand that wealth building is a marathon, not a sprint.

Now that we've covered my top real estate investing mistakes, I'd like to share some of my most memorable deals and blunders.

My First Investment Property: The Most Valuable Deal of My Investing Career

I purchased my first personal home in 1973. I was 21 years old at the time, and I sold the house 12 months later at a net profit of $4,000. That represented one-third of my income for the year. However, it wasn't until 1982 that I purchased my first investment property. I had been working in the cabinet manufacturing business and decided to partner with one of my co-managers to pursue a deal.

My buddy had attended a real estate investing seminar and was hot to buy his first property. We partnered up and bought our first investment property, but after several months of hard work, we sold it at a loss. That was undoubtedly the most profitable deal of my career. Why? Because my profit was gaining the understanding that I did not yet possess the tools necessary for success in real estate. Fast-forward 35 years, and I now have a pretty good idea of how to avoid these sorts of losses.

As it turns out, I was able to not only survive my mistake, but to earn a good living in this business and build a solid retirement income along the way. It was not an easy path, to be sure. You have to be resilient and determined to make it in this field.

In my opinion, there are three basic types of people. The first type are *the defeated*. The defeated do not learn from their mistakes. Next are *the average*. The average learn from their mistakes and plod on to mediocre success. (I put myself in the average category as I usually have to make the same mistake at least twice before learning from them.) Finally, we have *the wise*. The wise accomplish great things because they are capable of learning from the mistakes of others, which greatly accelerates their rise to success.

My First (and Last) "Subject-to" Deal

About twenty years ago, I went to hear a popular real estate guru speak. He was teaching a course on how to make big money by buying financed properties with non-assumable loans, and then reselling these houses to buyers who could put up the money for a down payment (but had credit scores too poor to qualify for a new loan). After hearing his lecture, I decided to give it a try.

I located a house about three houses down from the one I had grown up in. The house was owned by a Navy Seaman. He had purchased it with zero down on a VA loan. It was in average condition, but he owed about as much as the property was worth. He just wanted to sell it for his loan balance.

I followed the instructions in the course for doing a "subject-to" deal, and I did the paperwork to deed the house into a trust that I would control. It wasn't long before I found a buyer who paid me a $3,000 down payment and assumed my contract. I made a quick three grand and was a happy camper.

About a year later, I met the seller while standing in line at Pizza Hut's takeout counter. He recognized me first, walked over, and said (in language cleaned up to keep this G-rated): "I remember you. You're the SOB who stole my house. The guy you let buy it never made the first payment, but tore the property to pieces. I didn't have the money to fix it, so I had to let the lender foreclose and it ruined my credit. I trusted you, and you screwed me over."

I was mad at first, but the more I thought about, the more I realized he was right. For $3,000, I had really hurt this guy. I had told him I would handle everything and that selling to me was the best thing he could do. Yet I knew I had not lived up to my commitment. I could've rationalized that if I hadn't flipped his house in a subject-to deal, he probably would have lost it to the bank anyway. But that logic did nothing to ease my conscience. In that moment, I made the decision to never again do a subject-to deal.

Adam's Take on Mistakes

I can boil down my biggest mistakes in my real estate investing career into two categories. The first is not having become more active and not taking bigger risks when I was younger. If you are young and reading this, or if you are older but haven't built much of a net worth yet, then please listen to my call: Get out there right now and start doing some deals. There is no reason in the world why you can't do that. If you don't have a dollar to spare, then you don't have a dollar to lose.

At this point in my career, I have limited dollars to lose, so I normally try to put together deals that lower my risk and do not require me to put up large sums of cash or take on large risks. If I could turn back the clock and become my 19-year-old self again, I would take some serious risks, man! The upside of taking great risks is that you can end up earning great rewards. I'd learn the ropes the hard way, and it wouldn't matter either. I would still have plenty of time to learn how to do complicated deals, and I wouldn't have to worry about failing my family or not feeding my kids. If you're like me, though, and you have a family depending on you, you may want to be a little smarter about how you conduct your deals. Even if you are willing to take on more risk, you never want to conduct your deals recklessly.

And that leads me to category number two. If I could go back and amend my mistakes, one of the biggest things I would change is my hardheadedness. I would have listened to my mentors, and I would have done more of what they told me to do. After all, they were having great success, so why should I be able to do it better? I was learning how to do deals during a time when the internet was transforming business methods. People went from doing business in person and on the phone to conducting business via email and on social networks. Technology has revolutionized the way we live and the way we do business.

One thing that hasn't changed, though, is the way deals are analyzed and the way people collaborate to put deals together. All the time, I see novice investors who post deals for sale and then hide behind emails when my team asks them for a copy of the original contract. If this were 20 years ago, this investor would be sitting at a table in front of us looking very silly with no original contract in hand. In reality, these novice investors never had a contract. They went out and sold an idea, and now they're scrambling to get the original contract from the seller. Don't do this. Don't act bigger than you are. Conduct your real estate investing endeavors honestly, professionally, and in a timely manner. Never ignore the human factor of doing business with real people. The best deals have always been done sitting across the dinner table, and they always will be.

CHAPTER 18

Building Wealth with Real Estate

The term "real estate" is very inclusive. Houses, apartments, land, strip malls, and warehouses are all heralded under the real estate banner. Even when we consider houses exclusively, the term would encompass everything from shotgun shacks in war zones to multi-million-dollar oceanfront mansions. When I hear that real estate is up or real estate is down, it doesn't mean a lot to me. Even when you specifically identify an exact property, there are other factors involved. These factors include questions such as: When did you buy the property? Did you pay cash or leverage the deal with a loan? Have rents for the property increased, held steady, or declined? The truth is that no market can be accurately described as "good" or "bad." There is money to be made in any market, and savvy investors know how to make it.

The following is the progressive line of thinking and experience that has led me to my preferred market segment.

I choose to invest in real estate because…

1. I can buy homes substantially below market value from motivated, distressed sellers.
2. I can shelter earned income with depreciation, resulting in paying minimal income taxes.
3. I can control my investments, allowing me to improve their value.

4. Shelter is a basic human need, and land is limited due to scarcity, so there will always be a demand for real estate.

Until about 20 years ago, I had 100% of my retirement invested in mutual funds. I would check the fund values every few days to see if I was making or losing money. I don't know why I checked so often as I had no idea what I could do to influence my account values. Eventually, I moved that money into rental property, and I am so glad that I did. My retirement will now be about 4-5 times what it would have been if left in traditional investments.

With that in mind, I am going to tell you a brief and fun story that I wrote for you to help cement this mentality. The story is about two friends from the last ice age named Ug and Ook. I think you will find their story compelling as you learn the difference between earning an income in real estate investing versus building lasting wealth.

The Story of Ug and Ook

Ug and Ook were friends. It was 8,000 BC and life was difficult. They were hunters, and every time they got hungry, they had to kill something.

Ug was a very good hunter and provided for his family. His children followed his example. Now hunting was a difficult life—you have to move to follow the game and hope that you don't become the meal yourself. Ug aged quickly and soon had to be left behind on the hunts. His family hated to leave him, but hunting was all they knew. Ug was now barely surviving and soon realized that his children's future would probably be no better than his current reality.

Now Ook was also a hunter, but one day he made a life-changing discovery. He stepped on a seed that fell off a plant and that seed grew into food, plus provided more seeds. It took several years, but Ook's plants matured to the point that they provided food for him and his entire family. Ook was now a full-time farmer. He no longer had to hunt as his children had learned from his experience and now worked the farm. Ook and his wife built a little stone hut by the brook and lived a long and comfortable life. Neither Ook nor his children, nor his grandchildren, ever had to hunt again. They were able to trade their crops for everything they needed. Ook's small investment had changed his family's future forever!

Fast-forward 10,000 years or so. Ug's name has evolved into Doug and Ook's into Luke. Now Doug works a job that pays him enough to survive, but not enough to save (or so he thinks). He only has social security to depend on when he retires. His children followed his example and can't afford to help him very much. Doug and his wife eventually retire in a little Section 8-sponsored apartment. Life is okay, but Doug often looks back and wishes he had saved even a little bit and invested it. He is saddened by the fact that his children will probably wind up just like him, worried that social security might be broke by the time they need it.

Now Luke also worked a job, but he knew that he needed to control his own future, so he began to save 10% of his income. He drove used cars and cooked at home—whatever it took to get ahead. Soon Luke's nest egg had grown to a point where he could invest it. Luke got some good advice and invested in a house that he rented out. After a few years, Luke's tenant had paid off the property for him. Fast-forward 15 years, and Luke now owns enough houses that he no longer has to work. His rental income paid for his children's college education, and his example has inspired them. Luke gets depreciation tax write-offs from his real estate investments every year, which greatly reduces his tax burden while increasing his net worth. Luke will never sell his houses, but will leave them to his children. Luke hired a professional property manager so he and his wife could travel a lot, visit with the kids, and spend their time doing charity work. Luke even finds time to spend with his old friend Doug and hopes to teach him how to invest in real estate. Luke's small investment and discipline has changed his family's future forever!

Ug or Ook, Doug or Luke, hunter or farmer—the choice is yours. Choose wisely!

To sum up, let's take a closer look at why I've chosen to follow my particular path to real estate investing success.

I invest in residential rental houses because...

1. I can rent them out so that my tenants will actually pay for my investments.
2. I know single family houses. Commercial property is what I like to call "another animal." I only invest in markets that I understand.
3. Residential property values and occupancy rates are more predictable than commercial.
4. My risk is reduced by decentralization.

In my opinion, there is nothing that can be accomplished by investing in multifamily or commercial property that cannot be accomplished more easily and safely by investing in single family housing. I have met people who tell me that they are investing in houses now but want to "move up" to apartments. I answer with a question: "Is that so you can rent to a lower quality tenant and have all your investments tied up at a single location?"

I invest in low-middle income neighborhoods because...

1. It is the widest segment of the population.
2. I am positioned to get both move-up and move-down tenants.
3. I can invest smaller amounts as stand-alone investments, diversifying my risk.

4. Lower prices provide for lower leverage and associated risk.

I have owned homes in these areas for many years. Even in declining economic times, I always have renters. I have a buddy who owns more expensive houses in better areas. He asked me back in 2009 if I was experiencing as much difficulty finding tenants as he was. I answered, "No, the renters who can't afford your house anymore are now living in mine."

I only own "free and clear" or very low-leveraged houses because...

1. I never want to borrow more than 50% of the property's value.
2. I only want to borrow from individuals, with fully amortized loans that have payoff terms of 84 months or less.

It is ok to go into the bank, just stay off the carpet. I believe that if you need to raise money to invest, you should learn to borrow from private individuals. Remember: *You can afford to pay your friends and family a better rate than they'd earn by investing their money elsewhere.* I never borrow money to invest in real estate (or anything else) from banks or other institutional lenders. High leverage means high risk.

I only own fully-managed investments because...

1. A professional property manager does a much better job than I can.
2. I need to concentrate on building my portfolio, not dealing with tenants.

Do you really want to become a "landlord?" As I pointed out

earlier, most of the landlords I've met are not happy people. They have been "married" to their properties for so long that they've become sick of them. Most of them stop acquiring houses once they get to the point where they have no time to manage any more. If real wealth is your goal, hire a professional manager, and spend your time acquiring property and managing your actual investments instead of dealing with tenants. Learn to manage your overall investment business and portfolio and leverage the expertise of others for the daily management of "tenants and toilets."

To sum up, I believe that the ultimate investment is in bread and butter houses, located in lower middle-class working neighborhoods. These investment properties need to be owned free and clear, or financed with short-term, low-LTV, private loans—and they must be professionally managed. I do not invest in anything else, so my entire retirement is invested in this very specific market segment. Instead of wasting your time landlording or flipping houses to retail buyers, I would encourage you to become a "true" investor. I have actually built a substantial portion of my portfolio using some unique and exciting acquisition techniques that I developed a few years back. I share these techniques with my "Pathways" students. Flipping houses is a job, not an investment. I chose to make a living flipping rental property and to *build my future* by owning professionally managed residential housing.

Adam's Take on Building Wealth

If you want to keep working hard for your money and getting nowhere, then I recommend the following: Learn how to earn cash fast in real estate, and then spend that cash on a bigger house, a bright and shiny car, a beautiful boat, more expensive clothes, and anything else that will burn a big fat hole in your pocket. You can learn how to earn large sums of money by following one of the paths that Joe and I have shared in this book, and you can easily get to where you're consistently earning a six-figure income by joining our mentoring program. But I can tell you that the students who have joined us who love to spend money end up blowing all that cash on junk. The reality is that all the bright and shiny stuff you can buy with your hard-earned money is eventually going to rust, lose its fashion, and force you to spend time maintaining it—only to eventually break down in the end and turn into junk. The only way you stand a snowball's chance in hell of building wealth with real estate is if you *invest* that money.

My wife, Patricia, and I earned some pretty sweet cash before we had kids, but it didn't start out that way. She worked hard as a school teacher and earned peanuts slaving away every day with third graders. At night, when we both got home, we would have dinner and then she would grade papers. I can tell you I have witnessed firsthand how hard a young school teacher works and how little they get paid. She eventually got fed up with the low pay and decided to get her real estate license so she could sell houses on the weekend and bring in some extra cash.

The year that things started to pick up, I was working full-time running a property management business. I was also slaving away working hard on buying bank foreclosure deals for our family company, which we bought and sold to other investors. We did very well that year and had lots of cash to burn. The problem is we did burn through all our cash. We were burnt out each week from working so hard that we'd often order takeout during the week just to feed ourselves. If we did go to the grocery store, we would just buy whatever we felt we wanted or needed. On the weekends, it was party time. We had lavish dinner dates, expensive trips to other cities, and we attended any music concert we felt like going to—always buying the best seats. We wore expensive clothes, expensive jewelry, and we drove new cars that we financed for far too long.

I can remember one month when we threw a pool party at our home. An investor I was chatting with had told me if I was going to fill up my huge 25,000-gallon pool, I had better be smart enough to contact the local electric authority and submit the proper paperwork to ensure that I wasn't paying a huge water bill. I laughed and told him, "Jim, it's only water. How much can it really cost?" He looked at me like I was a dumb kid. Well, Jim, you were right. That month I received a $1,000 water bill, and that didn't even include the electricity we had carelessly burned through. Is any of this clicking for you? Are you burning through all your cash each month? Listen up good, please. The only way you are going to be able to build wealth with real estate is if you stop spending all your cash each month and start investing it into cash-producing real estate assets.

For our family, our preferred way of investing in real estate, as you know by now, is to buy affordable rental homes, fix them up, and then rent them out each month. We hire professionals to handle every part of the process. We even have assistants who locate the deals and get them to the closing table for us. After we close on the deals, we bring in our renovation crew to fix them up. When the renovation crew finishes, our property management company steps in and rents the home out to a qualified tenant. They deduct any rental repairs needed on the home, take out their 10% fee, and then send us the remaining funds each month—deposited directly into our bank account. Our property manager emails us our income statement for the month and is always a phone call away if we have any questions or concerns.

This method and process for buying and owning rental property has helped us build a cash-producing rental portfolio that averages a cash on cash net return of 15%. It has allowed us to build true wealth, and we are able to do it without having to invest much energy. We have built a team and mapped out a process for success, and you can do it too. It's going to take time and discipline to build your wealth, but you can surely do it. We are hoping you will take the best measures to ensure your future success, and we will be cheering for you the entire way.

Follow This Formula to Build Wealth with Real Estate

I am going to give you a tool and cheat sheet that you can use each and every month to help you build wealth with real estate. I stole part of this formula from financial genius Dave Ramsey. We attended his Financial Peace University a few years ago, and it really helped us solve some debt and savings problems we were having. We got back on track to saving our cash and investing it into our family's future. Before I share my formula with you, I want to share Dave's method for financial success. Dave believes "there is a process for winning with money over time. No matter where you are today, whether you're financially secure or financially distressed, these Baby Steps will walk you step by step toward financial peace."

So, here are Dave Ramsey's 7 Baby Steps:

1. Save $1,000 in a beginner emergency fund.
2. Pay off all your credit cards and debt by using the snowball method of paying off your smallest debts first, and then paying off the next larger debt until all your debts are paid off (except your primary residence). You pay off the smallest debts first due to the psychological effect it creates within your brain of winning the victory of paying off debts.
3. Put 3-6 months of expenses into savings.
4. Invest 15% of your household income into Roth IRAs and pre-tax retirement plans.

5. Save for your children's college education using tax-favored plans.
6. Pay off your house early.
7. Build wealth and give!

Here is the formula I was able to develop after attending Dave's university:

Develop Emergency Fund + Pay Off All Credit Cards and Short-Term Debts + 3 Months Savings Net + Kids' College Savings Fund + Invest 15% of Income into Self-Directed Roth IRA + Purchase Affordable Rental Homes = Maximum Wealth Building

So, my plan is to follow Dave's 7 Baby Steps and then invest my money into our affordable rental homes. I also plan to spend a considerable amount of my time in the future working with charities and helping build houses, schools, churches, and orphanages in Haiti. Well, that's my plan for wealth building, financial success, and happiness in my marriage and life. I hope you will spend some time mapping out your budget, saving some cash to invest, and then purchasing some affordable rental homes to bring in consistent income for growing your nest egg.

CHAPTER 19

The Importance of Networking

Networking is, of course, a great way to meet other investors and professionals in the industry. That being said, when you are out there networking, I want you to be careful. More to the point, I want you to be aware of sharks and clowns.

In Chapter 2, I spoke about the importance of building a customer base. When I began building our current customer base, there was no Facebook, no Twitter, and no LinkedIn. I was also on my own, and as the internet was fairly new, there was no instruction manual. At the time, I had just left my job, so I did not have a lot of time to spare. I needed buyers and I needed them immediately.

My first step was to buy a simple "canned" website where I could post my deals for sale. Next, I purchased a long-term ad in the investment property section of the local newspaper. The ad read: "To buy houses at REAL wholesale prices, visit www.joelocklear. com." This brought me some activity, but alone, it was not sufficient to produce enough buyers to move all of the properties that I could contract to buy.

My next move was to join the local real estate club, attend every meeting, and volunteer at every opportunity. I became a teacher and a board member within a year, and later the education director and vice president. I eventually served as president for several years, but serving within this group was both time consuming and frustrating. This club was run by an elected board of directors and, unfortunately, having real estate investing knowledge or leadership ability were not qualifications for board membership.

However, my involvement with this club was well worth the effort. In a short period of time, I had more buyers than I could supply with houses. Many of my vendors, partners, lenders, and buyers were obtained as a direct benefit of participating in various investing clubs and networking groups. My advice to you is to join your local Real Estate Investors Association and/or other local networking groups. Promote your business, write a few articles for the news-letters, volunteer if you have time, but avoid becoming part of the political leadership.

Since my son Adam joined me as partner, marketing has been a breeze. All I have to do is write out exactly how I think our mar-keting plan should be implemented and email it to him. Adam will then email me right back with a note saying, "Dad, I love you, but marketing is my job. Stay out of it! The world has changed and you're still living in the stone age." I hate to admit it, but he's right. With the advent of digital marketing, blogs, YouTube, webcasts, and squeeze pages, it is a new marketing world out there, and Adam has mastered it. Although he has harnessed technology to elevate our marketing to the next level, Adam still agrees with me that networking and local marketing are indispensable when building a successful and sustainable real estate investing business.

Before I wrap up, I'd like to impart one final piece of wisdom when it comes to both local and online networking...

Beware of Sharks and Clowns!

When you're out there networking, you need to be aware of sharks and clowns. The real estate investing business is virtually infested with both. The sharks are out to get you, and you will find these scammers anywhere there is money to be made. Sharks are class-A predators. They don't see you as a customer, they see you as "lunch." The sharks are experts at luring you in, dazzling you with dreams of wealth, and then picking your pocket clean. The only limitation to their interest in you is the depth of your pocket. Here are a few tell-tale signs of a real estate investor education shark:

1. They concentrate on selling you the "dream." Keep an ear out for rhetoric with very little substance.
2. They tend to oversimplify things. Terms like "foolproof," and phrases like "so simple anybody can do it" and "you can buy real estate without money" are the stock in trade for these types of sharks.
3. They concentrate on the hook. Many of the educational gurus will make you an offer that is only good for a very limited time. This is a ploy to get you to pull out your wallet before carefully considering your purchase.

To root out the sharks, ask yourself a simple question: If their claim of making millions in the real estate business is true, and anybody can do it, then why are they concentrating on selling education? If their claims were true, couldn't they just hire a bunch of employees to follow their "system," pay them nicely, and keep the millions in profit for themselves?

Now, please don't misunderstand my position on buying education. There are many legitimate and excellent educators out there selling an honest product. The majority of the legitimate gurus are those who have been successful in the investing business and have established a passive income, allowing them to now enjoy life and pass on to others the business they love. Yes, they make money selling education, but it is *real* education—not the fluffed-up gimmickry peddled by the sharks.

With that said, not all of the sharks are educators. Many of them are investors. I once met an investor who had a reputation as a real "go-getter." He was boastful and asinine. Later on, I found out later he had gotten into trouble for selling property that he knew was located over a sink hole. Unfortunately, sharks are everywhere in the real estate investing business. If you are going into these waters, you need to learn how to recognize them. Going to lunch is fun. Being lunch is not.

Now, the sharks are dangerous, but the clowns can do just as much damage. While the sharks know who and what they are, the clowns don't have a clue. Clowns include the "newbies" who want to tell you how to make big money, but don't have two nickels to rub together. Most clowns suffer from "paralysis of analysis." They have studied and studied, but their fear of failure has kept them on the sidelines. These clowns are a wealth of knowledge, but devoid of wisdom. Listen to them at your own peril.

The best method of identifying a clown is to simply ask them to verify their actual success. How many deals have they closed in the last six months? What are the addresses of the deals they worked on and business names that they closed on? The number of deals will be identifiable in the county records. Perhaps the most dangerous of all is what I call the "hybrid." The hybrid begins life as a clown, but after years of book learning and moderate success, decides he or she has arrived. Swayed by the dream of becoming the next great guru, they step out of the clown suit, grow teeth, strap on a fin, and slide into the kiddy pool.

Adam recently called my attention to one of my former students who was now offering mentoring to newbie real estate investors. Now, I know this "mentor," and I am familiar with his level of expertise and his true accomplishments. His mentoring price was $20,000. If he offered me his services for free, I would decline. I believe that this guy began with honest intentions, achieved moderate success, and was lured into the guru business by dreams of grandeur. An unqualified educator or mentor can kill your investing career before it gets started.

The best advice I can give you is to spend the necessary time and effort analyzing your own assets and abilities before considering buying expensive education and mentoring. Once you have identified your specific educational needs, search for educators who can verify their experience and give you the exact education that YOU have determined you need. Make sure to speak to others not associated with the educator. A little research up front can save you a lot of money and, more importantly, help move you along your chosen path to success.

In summary, every business has sharks and clowns. Every business also has real educators with verifiable track records who offer honest education and mentoring. These proven performers can be recognized by their lack of lofty rhetoric and their willingness to tell you both the good and the bad of their investing specialty. Networking is a great way to meet many new businesses and strategic partners that can help you learn how to invest in real estate and get better at what you are doing. Please be careful, and remember: If it sounds too good to be true, it probably is.

Adam's Take on Networking

When I think about networking, I always think about my good friend and business broker Kim Deas. You see, Kim is what I would call a "networking queen." She has attended nearly every networking event in our city twice. Kim has discovered something that many professionals and real estate investors take for granted: that nothing replaces a face-to-face interaction. You could spend the next 12 months, and $30,000 from your marketing budget, trying to build up quality leads that Kim could generate in just 30 days from net-working and shaking hands. She will beat you every time due to the fact that she will get right in front of her prospects and let them get to know her a little before they do any business with her.

Networking also gets you out in the professional community and gives you the opportunity to become known for something. Most of the people you meet will not become your long-term clients, but some of them will. The best part about becoming known for what you do is people will begin to refer other professionals they know to you. They'll also refer friends and family once they trust you. This is when your real estate investing endeavors will really take off. Just be careful with this tactic because it works so well that leads will roll in on top of leads. Once this happens, you will run out of time and be forced to expand your business. It's a great problem to have, I just want you to be ready for it.

10 Tips to Maximize Your Networking Success
1. Get out of your normal circles.
2. Dress for success.
3. Differentiate your business card.
4. Do not act overtly saleslike.
5. Always ask yourself why you are there.
6. Work the room.
7. Let others talk first and then react.
8. Become known for what you do.
9. Stay consistent.
10. Hone in on the best events for you in your area.

Once You Master Networking, Take It to the Next Level
After you learn how to gain clients and influence others, you may decide to move forward and begin to teach others what you have

learned. This is where Joe and I are now in our careers. We love giving back, and we love educating other investors on how to get deals done correctly and how to avoid the pitfalls in this business. We have a real estate investor Meetup group that we run in Jacksonville that, as of this writing, has grown to nearly 2,000 investors. By the time you read this, I'm sure we will be much larger as we get hundreds of new members each and every month.

Joe and I fully believe teaching is the highest form of learning. It also puts you in a position where you can be the expert in the room. If you can learn how to become the featured speaker at a networking event, you will see your business sales explode in volume. I have read and practiced many different marketing methods in an attempt to gain traction with my real estate investment businesses. Over the years, I've tried a variety of marketing strategies—everything from Google ads, Facebook ads, retargeting ads, and boosting posts on Facebook to direct mail, podcasts, YouTube training videos, email marketing, blogging, cold calls, flyers, and more. But the one marketing strategy that has converted more prospects into paying clients than all the others combined is networking.

Networking will help you fast-track your success in gaining clients. It's very important that you develop a system for measuring how you define success in marketing. I define success for my turn-key real estate investment business as follows: *How many houses did I actually sell from the amount of energy and dollars that I spent on the marketing campaign?* It's very important that you are able to measure the energy and money spent on each of your marketing campaigns.

Let's look at an example. Let's say I spent 30 minutes of my time writing an advertisement for Facebook. In this scenario, I set a budget of $100 and served the ad to 500 people over a 30-day period. Let's assume that I converted 10 of those viewers and got them to sign up for my private email list, and one of those email subscribers actually bought a house from me. So my conversion rate based on the 500 viewers would be 2%. However, once I got them on my email list, the conversion rate jumps to 10%, since 1 out of 10 new email subscribers purchased a home from me.

In reality, the numbers may not be as good as this scenario, and it may take me some time to develop a relationship with my email subscriber before they purchase a house from me. To be honest, what I really want to do is get them on my email list and then invite them to my real estate investor networking event, where they'll see me in a room with a large number of attendees who are all asking me questions since I'm the expert in the room.

We have learned that if you are running the networking event, or if you're a featured speaker, your conversions go way up. You can easily skip the online ads and go straight to the source. The key to getting people to find you is what we call *inbound marketing*. So, you start your own real estate networking group, you begin holding events in your local market, and then eventually word of mouth travels and attendees show up. You can run some online ads too, but you shouldn't have to spend much here. Just list your networking event on one of the online event websites in your area. When your attendees arrive, you network with them, educate them, and get them on your mailing list. You will sell far more houses relative to the amount of money and energy you put into it than if you were to run ads and send people to your website.

It's important that you give your attendees some value for coming to your meetings. Whether you give them a free class, free advice, or vendor resources, you need to give them a reason to show up. They need a reason to tell a friend why they should attend the next event. Networking is the most powerful form of marketing Joe and I have found for our real estate investment companies. I strongly recommend, at a minimum, that you consistently attend your local real estate investor meetings, and if you really want to take things to the next level, consider launching and running your own networking events.

CHAPTER 20

Stepping Out of Your Chosen Path

Now that you have analyzed your assets, abilities, and time frames—
and chosen a specific path through the real estate investor maze—it's
time to get started. Let's take a look at what you need to do next.

Step 1—Get Educated

Now that you have chosen your path, you need to learn everything you can about the real estate investing technique you will use.
Remember, as a new investor, you must master one area at a time,
so don't waste time and money trying to learn "everything about
real estate." Diluting your education at the outset is a major mistake.
Focus on your beginning path only and your chance of success will
be greatly enhanced.

Before spending a penny on education, do your research and talk
with other investors who have purchased a package from this educator. Once you've determined your beginning pathway, you should
hone in on education specific to it. About 20 years ago, I bought
a specialized education package on marketing to find motivated
sellers. This educational package was phenomenal, and I still use the
techniques I learned. The key is that I knew *exactly* what I needed,
then sought out the premier expert on the subject and bought his
package. I cannot remember how much the information cost, but
I can promise you that my return on investment is off the charts!

Step 2—Find a Mentor

I never had an official mentor, however, I have received a lot of mentoring. I have a close friend named Tom who lived next door to a person that is now one of the most successful marketers of real estate education in America. I am not going to mention this guru's name as I don't want to seek his permission. I can tell you that the first time I went to Tom's home, about 30 years ago, the guru's front yard was filled with broken-down carnival rides. Tom is a great guy and loves to talk about what he does and what his friend taught him. Anytime I needed advice, I would ask Tom. To this day, I still do business with and consult with Tom. He is one of the few people in Jacksonville who has as much hands-on renovation experience as I do.

One of the best places to locate a mentor is at your local real estate investor club. Consider trading your labor for mentoring, but make sure that your mentor is qualified in the specific field you have chosen. If you can't afford personal mentoring, find a "virtual" mentor. Search out the experts in your chosen field and read everything you can find written by them.

The first time I agreed to mentor a beginning investor, the student lived in Tampa, Florida. Christian was a good student and did exactly as I taught him. Our deal was that he would come to Jacksonville for one week and stay in my home. I took him with me everywhere and taught him exactly how I operated. After the week was up, Christian was to return to Tampa, follow my instructions, and then send me half of his first six months' earnings. In month three, I received a check for a little over $12,000. Christian learned in just a few short months how to earn a decent living from doing real estate deals that took me a decade to learn how to do. He was driven, humble, and ready to listen to his mentor. His success carried on for many years after I mentored him.

Step 3—Create Your Business Plan
Just refer back to Chapter 13 and complete your business plan.

You will not likely be able to achieve long-term success without one. I recommend putting together a basic business plan first, and then expanding and creating a more detailed version as time goes on.

Step 4—Do a Deal

I can still remember my first summer camp. It was a Boy's Club day camp at Camp Stratton in Hilliard, Florida. Soon after arrival, we decked out in swim shorts and met at the shallow end of the lake. There was a floating raft out in the deeper water, and the purpose of the exercise was to separate the swimmers from the non-swimmers. The swimmers got their run of the lake and the non-swimmers were confined to a roped-off area where they were closely watched by a lifeguard. I knew that I couldn't swim a lick, but when my turn came to swim to the raft, I jumped right in. Kicking, flailing, and gurgling, I got about halfway to the raft when a lifeguard had to drag me out. I set foot back on land, belittled by the laughter of my fellow non-swimmers. As I sat down amongst them, the lifeguard barked at me: "What are you doing? Get over there with the swimmers!" Then he went on to say, "Half of learning to swim is overcoming the fear of drowning. You'll be swimming by tomorrow." I virtually "backed" over to the swimmers' group so my non-swimming friends could see my grin. I knew that I didn't really belong with the jocks in the swimmers' group, but I also knew that I would never again fear jumping in and giving it my best shot.

You cannot learn to swim by reading a book or sitting on the diving board. The same is true of real estate investing. Do the necessary preparation, but sooner or later you have to jump into the water and actually do your first deal. If you break even, that is fantastic! I lost $1,000 on my first deal, and, to this day, it remains the most valuable transaction of my real estate investing career.

Step 5—Rinse, Repeat, and Learn from Your Mistakes

More than likely, you're going to make some mistakes while doing your first deal. I know I have learned much about how to organize my deals, how to increase my profits, and how to decrease the time and energy I put into each project by doing actual deals. The more deals you do, the more you will learn. After you complete your second deal and you get that paycheck, I want you to reflect back and make a list of what was worth doing in that deal and what was not. Eventually, you will discover your style and niche, as well as your favorite types of deals. Keep doing deals and keep learning from your mistakes and you will be on the fast-track to becoming a successful real estate investor.

Adam's Take on Stepping Out

It's finally time to step out and do something with the path you have chosen. Like Joe said, the only way you will ever achieve any form of success is to go out and do something. Maybe you have never done a deal and you need more information and time to carve out your path. If that's the case, then I want you to flip to the back of the book when you finish reading and access some of the resources we have waiting for you there. Joe and I can help you get comfortable choosing the best path for you.

If you are comfortable enough to choose a path now, or if you are already working one of the paths and simply want to increase your sales and productivity, we would love to help. As we've said earlier, a good mentor can show you how to make your chosen path and strategy an absolute success. Just visit the provided resources, and we will get started building your customized strategy and business plan for success.

As you know, I started learning about real estate investing when I was 17. If I could go back in time and teach my younger self a thing or two, I would tell him to figure out *exactly* what he thinks he would be good at and what he would enjoy doing the most. I would also encourage him to go out and do just that. It is absolutely paramount that you choose to do things in life that you *enjoy* doing. Find people in the world who share in the pleasure of doing those same things, and build win-win scenarios and win-win relationships. You will need the high-level support and encouragement that these all-star partners can provide for you. Once you start doing deals, apply this same mentality if you want to enjoy your life and achievements.

I can tell you as time went on, and as I matured in the deals I was doing, I learned to stay away from highly stressful transactions. I also eventually got to a point in my career and life where I refused to work with grumpy people. Grumpy people usually will ask for too much of your time, and they only think of themselves when you do deals together. The truth is, no one wants to be miserable, so they will search for ways to fill their happiness cup. If their happiness cup is low, they will steal your time and do things like talk about themselves too much, or they will lead you on and eventually cut you out of the deal to earn a higher profit.

We previously spoke about sharks and clowns and the hybrid version of the two. I want to end this chapter by adding a fourth person to be careful of. Watch out for grumpy people. They will ruin your deals and complicate your life. They will steal your happiness and dump it into their own cup. If it's not going to be fun, in my humble opinion, it sure as heck isn't worth wasting your time and energy on. There are so many happy, loving, motivated, and honest people out there in the world. They would love to put together a win-win real estate investment deal with you. So, your first order of business when stepping out onto your chosen path is to track them down and do some great business together. I can promise you it will feel a whole lot better when you do, and life will be so much more rewarding in real estate investing and beyond!

CHAPTER 21

The Secret Revealed

By now, you have probably guessed that the "Secret to Real Estate Investing" is the simple fact that *there is no secret*!
Real estate investing is a business and it's subject to all of the basics of operating any successful company. There are many details, pathways, and sub-pathways, and making the best choices for your business will be imperative to your success.

Having taught thousands of new investors over the past 30 years, I have heard many of them say things like "I want to invest in homes that I can sell for a good profit'" or "I want to buy houses that are easy to finance." When I ask them why, I seldom get a coherent answer. The truth is, they are simply repeating what someone else has told them. They're convinced that the techniques they have been taught will work, and I agree with them. Almost every technique *will* work, but there are two questions you need to ask yourself: *Will the technique work for me*, and *will it allow me to meet my goals within my targeted time frame*?

Almost every educator presents the pathway that he or she is selling as the best method available for you to reach your goals. They tell you that it is so simple that anyone can do it. Next, they will paint a picture of their rise from humble beginnings to fantastic wealth. Finally, they'll tell you about all the waitresses and auto mechanics who got rich following their investing system. Does this story sound familiar?

I am not telling you that these educators are being misleading, or even that they are exaggerating. I will, however, tell you this. In my 30+ years of associating with the real estate education business, I have yet to hear one educator actually ask a prospective customer about their personal assets, abilities, or time frames. The gurus promote their methods as the best thing out there, and they will sell their system to anyone with money to buy it.

The good news is that you can achieve fantastic success and build substantial wealth within the real estate investing business. Now I cannot promise you success, but I can promise you the following: If you begin with an open mind and you are willing to spend the time and effort up front to analyze your abilities, assets, goals, and time frames, then you will be able to choose a "pathway" that will give you the greatest chance of success.

Adam and I want to begin by teaching you how to determine the investing method that is best for *you*. We will never choose a path for you. However, we will provide you with enough information and guidance to allow you to make an educated choice for yourself. That is what this book and our Pathways education series is all about.

This book is a simple "primer." There is a lot more to learn! Adam and I have developed a very comprehensive education program that will not only give you a solid foundation on real estate investing, but it'll also teach you the advanced insider information *specific* to your chosen pathway.

In parting, I would like to talk with you directly and frankly. Adam and I have built a business locating, remodeling, and selling investment houses to hands-off investors. This business is our "job," not our future. I understand that many of you will want to choose a beginning path that will give you a quick income boost. That is where I began and I still operate there today. I have, however, made substantial investment in my family's future along the way.

Be careful of thinking that you will begin by flipping property and *later* invest your excess earnings in ownership. In reality, many investors simply spend their newfound income to raise their standard of living. I implore you to learn to build for your future from the very beginning!

It is passive income from my portfolio of low-cost single family rentals that is allowing me to decrease my daily street-level real estate activity and do more of what I enjoy most. I love fishing, writing, riding my Harley, and teaching you to become a successful real estate investor. I would encourage you not to start with just "making money" but to invest as much as you can early on. If you can make it a habit from day one, you will be able to easily build true wealth.

I'd like to point out that my success does not dwell within my bank account. It lies in the fact that I am going to be financially stable and able to enjoy the rest of my life without worrying about income. I will leave a healthy inheritance to my three sons as well as an example of entrepreneurship, leadership, and fair and honest dealing.

Adam's Final Words

It's true, there is no formal secret to real estate investing. It's a large industry with lots of emotions flying around that people just can't help but complicate.

One of the things Joe and I have tried to emulate over the years is to keep things simple. The acronym KISS has been used by many different motivational speakers, trainers, and mentors over the years. You need to "Keep It Simple, Silly" when it comes to doing deals and carving out your chosen real estate investment path.

It's this mentality that enables Joe and I to continue to mold our businesses and ventures into cash-producing machines. Our secret to success has been to heavily focus on the path we are traveling at the current time. It's too hard to do more than one thing at a time when you haven't mastered your current path yet. To master our current path, we developed a solid system to partially automate our workflow and then maximize our profits. We will eventually find a path that enables us to reduce the time and energy we spend on menial tasks in order to focus on more important or complicated tasks that only we can do.

In the end, it's up to you to discover your own path and unlock your personal secret for real estate investing success. It's a journey that will require risks, an entrepreneurial spirit, and a willingness to learn and get your hands dirty. The good news is it's absolutely fulfilling and so very invigorating. I can't imagine being locked in a cubicle each day or working a structured desk job. Being a real estate investor is the best job on earth. I hope you will take the next steps and join us on the journey.

The Man in the Arena

The following quote is from Theodore Roosevelt. We have used these words to end our educational classes for years. We believe it's a great quote that helps motivate our students to get active with their real estate investing endeavors.

> "It is not the critic who counts; not the man who points out how the strong man stumbles, or where the doer of deeds could have done them better. The credit belongs to the man who is actually in the arena, whose face is marred by dust and sweat and blood; who strives valiantly; who errs, who comes short again and again, because there is no effort without error and shortcoming; but who does actually strive to do the deeds; who knows great enthusiasms, the great devotions; who spends himself in a worthy cause; who at the best knows in the end the triumph of high achievement, and who at the

worst, if he fails, at least fails while daring greatly, so that
his place shall never be with those cold and timid souls who
neither know victory nor defeat."

Excerpt from the speech "Citizenship in a Republic"
delivered at the Sorbonne, in Paris, France
on 23 April, 1910

Today is the only day that you have. Yesterday is gone forever
and tomorrow never comes. What will you do *today* to change your
future, and the future of your children and grandchildren forever?
We hope that what you have learned in this book will help motivate
you along your path to real estate success.

Best Regards,
Joe & Adam

RESOURCES

1. http://locklearpartners.com
This is an example of what a turn-key real estate provider website can look like. We have used it for the past five years to grow our buyers list and attract turn-key buyers. We purposely do not post deals for sale on our site. The deals are so good we can't keep them in inventory!

2. https://www.meetup.com/JAX-REIM/
A few years back, we decided to put together our own group of real estate investors. This group meets monthly in our hometown of Jacksonville, Florida. We network, share stories, provide market updates, and do actual deals together every month. Come on out and meet us or start your own local group in your own city.

3. https://www.upwork.com
This is the best website we have found to locate, interview, and hire virtual assistants. You can also get help with logo design, website design, search engine optimization, marketing, and so much more. Check it out!

4. https://www.aweber.com
We have been in love with AWeber's email marketing services for the past 15 years. When you choose your email provider, it's paramount that they can get you past the spam filters. AWeber understands this very well and their entire platform is built on this mentality. What good is an email service if you end up in the spam or social folder?

5. https://www.daveramsey.com

Dave Ramsey taught us a thing or two after we started earning big paychecks. The danger you face as you begin to accumulate your wealth is the temptation to blow a lot of it. Believe it or not, many very wealthy people end up with serious debt problems. Dave Ramsey can teach you how to budget correctly and keep the money you have earned. Every entrepreneur needs to learn how to save up for a rainy day and properly manage his money. Learn Dave's simple lessons and you will be set for years of financial success!

Thanks so much for reading our book. We hope to see you out there doing deals very soon!

Joe & Adam

MY NOTES

MY NOTES

Do You Want to Learn from Joe and Adam in a Private Setting?

Joe and Adam provide professional real estate investor mentoring to a handful of select students who are motivated to succeed and change their financial future forever. A few years ago, Joe was approached by a small group of students after one of his monthly educational speaking engagements. This small group had only just gotten to know one another during the last national real estate investor event that had come through town, and they were hanging out trying to learn from each other. They told us they were eager to get started with real estate investing, and, after attending the event, they were motivated, but they just could not justify the $40,000 in fees that the guru wanted to charge them. I think our hearts broke a little that day, and we decided we would take a stand against these national media-infused real estate educators and provide top-notch, street-level education and personal mentoring for the average Joe. It was aimed at those who simply couldn't afford an Ivy League education or come up with that much cash to get started in real estate investing. Three months later, we launched *Real Investor Mentors*, with a focus on helping new and seasoned investors get on the right path for success. Since then, we have educated and mentored over 1,000 students, helping them get their real estate investing careers off the ground. Our students and apprentices have conducted thousands of deals, and some of them have even quit their day jobs to become full-time real estate investors. Many others have simply developed high-yield rental portfolios, earned tons of cash doing profitable deals, and become very successful following our techniques to put together win-win deals.

So, what do you say? Are you ready to learn from Joe and Adam?

**Visit:
realinvestormentors.com**

Change Your Family's Future Forever!

www.ingramcontent.com/pod-product-compliance
Lightning Source LLC
Chambersburg PA
CBHW070924210326
41520CB00021B/6795